NONPROFIT ESSENTIALS

:cruiting and

ing Fundraising

Volunteers

NONPROFIT ESSENTIALS

Recruiting and Training Fundraising Volunteers

Linda Lysakowski, ACFRE

WILEY

John Wiley & Sons, Inc.

Library of Congress Cataloging-in-Publication Data:

ISBN-13 978-0-471-70648-9
ISBN-10 0-471-70648-5

Printed in the United States of America

10 9 8 7 6 5 4 3 2 1

For my husband Marty,
the wind beneath my wings.

The AFP Fund Development Series

The AFP Fund Development Series is intended to provide fund development professionals and volunteers, including board members (and others interested in the nonprofit sector), with top-quality publications that help advance philanthropy as voluntary action for the public good. Our goal is to provide practical, timely guidance and information on fundraising, charitable giving, and related subjects. The Association of Fundraising Professionals (AFP) and Wiley each bring to this innovative collaboration unique and important resources that result in a whole greater than the sum of its parts. For information on other books in the series, please visit:

http://www.afpnet.org

The Association of Fundraising Professionals

The Association of Fundraising Professionals (AFP) represents 26,000 members in more than 170 chapters throughout the world, working to advance philanthropy through advocacy, research, education, and certification programs. The association fosters development and growth of fundraising professionals and promotes high ethical standards in the fundraising profession. For more information or to join the world's largest association of fundraising professionals, visit *www.afpnet.org*.

2004–2005 AFP Publishing Advisory Committee

Linda L. Chew, CFRE, Chair
Associate Director, Alta Bates Summit Foundation

Nina P. Berkheiser, CFRE
Director of Development, SPCA of Pinellas County

D. C. Dreger, ACFRE
Senior Campaign Director, Custom Development Systems (CDS)

Samuel N. Gough, CFRE
Principal, The AFRAM Group

Audrey P. Kintzi, ACFRE
Chief Advancement Officer, Girl Scout Council St. Croix Valley

Robert Mueller, CFRE
Vice President, Hospice Foundation of Louisville

Maria Elena Noriega
Director, Noriega Malo & Associates

Leslie E. Weir, MA, ACFRE
Director of Gift Planning, Health Sciences Centre Foundation

Sharon R. Will, CFRE
Director of Development, South Wind Hospice

John Wiley & Sons

Susan McDermott
Editor (Professional/Trade Division), John Wiley & Sons

AFP Staff

Jan Alfieri
Manager, New Product Development, AFP

Walter Sczudlo
Executive Vice President & General Counsel

Acknowledgments

I would like to thank all my clients and associates who contributed to this book including Sue Kreeger, CFRE; Ellen Arnold, CFRE; and Kurt Mische; and Shanon Hafer for assisting with formatting the manuscript. I would also like to thank my colleagues at the Association of Fundraising Professionals (AFP) for their encouragement and assistance in developing the concept for this book, especially Cathlene Williams, Ph.D. and Jan Alfieri.

Most especially I want to thank Ellen Ayoub for her invaluable help, many hours of time, and expert guidance in reviewing the manuscript, proofreading, and assisting with the chapter layout.

About the Author

Linda Lysakowski (Las Vegas, Nevada) is the President/CEO of Capital Venture, a consulting and training firm specializing in capital and endowment campaigns and other fundraising services. She is one of the first 55 people worldwide to hold the Advanced Certified Fundraising Executive designation. Linda was named Eastern Pennsylvania's "Outstanding Fundraising Executive of the Year" in 2001, and in 2004 received this same recognition from the Las Vegas Chapter of AFP. A magna cum laude graduate of Alvernia College, Linda is also a graduate of AFP's Faculty Training Academy. She has been a speaker at local, regional, and national fundraising conferences for more than 10 years. She has authored three booklets in the AFP Ready Reference Series (*Establishing Your Development Office, Getting Ready for a Capital Campaign,* and *Building an Effective Board of Directors*) as well as articles for related newsletters and other nonprofit publications (*Charity Channel, CASE Currents, International Journal of Nonprofit and Voluntary Sector Marketing*).

Contents

Introduction

After many years in the fundraising arena as a volunteer, a staff person, a board member, and a consultant, I discovered a recurring theme of all the organizations in which I've been involved. The degree of success an organization demonstrated in involving volunteers in its fundraising efforts had a direct relationship with the success of its fundraising efforts.

It became apparent to me that volunteers not only played a critical role in the fundraising programs of successful organizations, but that volunteering in the fundraising arena often led to a career in philanthropy. Many of the development professionals I spoke with over the years started their own career as a volunteer—including myself! A "recovering" banker, I first got involved in development as a volunteer for my college's annual corporate fundraising appeal. As I became more involved with the college and its fundraising efforts, I realized I was in the wrong profession and accepted my first development position as Assistant Vice President of Institutional Advancement at my alma mater, bringing with me the perspective and experience of a volunteer fundraiser.

After years of working with staff and volunteers in fundraising, I realized that the development profession has a great deal to gain by encouraging the involvement of volunteer fundraisers. The relationship between a donor and a volunteer can enhance the whole philanthropic arena. And staff and volunteers together can do great things for their organizations and, even more importantly, for the donor.

The importance of volunteers in fundraising has been well recognized by the world's largest organization of professional fundraisers. Each year the Association of Fundraising Professionals honors an outstanding volunteer fundraiser. During National Philanthropy Day, many local chapters also honor an outstanding fundraising volunteer. However, little has been written about the relationship of donors, professional staff, and volunteer fundraisers.

It is in the best interest of all development professionals to learn more about the techniques to be used in recruiting and training volunteers in order for them to be effective fundraisers. It is my hope that this book will help professional fundraisers understand the importance of volunteer fundraisers, how they can involve volunteers in all the aspects of their development programs, where to find fundraising volunteers, how to recruit these volunteers, and how to assure that they will stay involved with their organization.

CHAPTER 1

Why and How to Use Volunteers in Fundraising

 After reading this chapter, you will be able to:

- List the reasons why people volunteer to do fundraising.
- List the qualities to look for in volunteer fundraisers.
- List various fundraising activities in which you can use volunteers.

"The American tradition of philanthropy is built on the foundation of volunteerism and that tradition must not be lost," says James Greenfield in his book *Fundraising*, second edition. In the United States, where voluntary action has been such a strong part of the philanthropic process, volunteer fundraisers have been recognized as an integral part of the profession of fundraising. Volunteers in the United States have been involved in fundraising as early as colonial days, when Benjamin Franklin set about the task of raising money for charitable organizations. In other parts of the world, where fundraising is an emerging profession, the role of volunteers is even more critical.

Many development officers struggle with these questions: Is it easier to just do it oneself? Who should make the ask—paid staff or volunteers? Can volunteers be as effective as staff in making the ask? Who can be recruited to serve as volunteer fundraisers? How do these volunteers receive the training and information they need to be effective fundraisers? If staff members are the professionals, why does an organization need volunteers for its fundraising efforts? The answers to these questions will vary from organization to organization, but almost every nonprofit organization benefits from involving volunteers in more of their fundraising activities. The key is learning how to recruit the right volunteers for the right job and providing those volunteers with the tools they need in order to be effective fundraisers.

In her book *Pinpointing Affluence*, Judith Nichols says that volunteers are the best advocates for an organization. "They provide the community's endorsement for your nonprofit, encouraging people of affluence and influence to follow their lead." As Nichols explains, it is important for a nonprofit to prove its credibility by showing the ability to recruit volunteer fundraisers. Equally as important as the advantages to the organization of involving volunteers are the benefits to the volunteer fundraisers. Nichols quotes Maurice Gurin in stating that, "In soliciting large gifts, volunteers derive the kind of satisfaction that increases their own interests and commitment. Depriving them of that satisfaction could well have serious consequences for fundraising and for philanthropy in general."

Why Do People Volunteer?

In *The Seven Faces of Philanthropy*, Russ Alan Prince and Karen Maru File talk about seven types of people and what motivates each to give: Altruist, Communitarian, Devout, Investor, Socialite, Repayer, and Dynast. Altruists give (or volunteer) purely for the sake of being able to help. Communitarians contribute their time, talent, and treasure to a cause they feel will make their community a better place in which to live and because they truly care about their community.

Religious beliefs often play a significant role in people's propensity to give a gift or to volunteer their time, as in the case of the Devouts. Investors are more likely to make a gift of time or money if they feel there is some payback for themselves or others. Socialites are often the donors, or volunteers, who are seen at events where they can mix and mingle with other like-minded people. Repayers give of their time and/or money because they feel the need to give something back to society, or more specifically to an organization that has helped them, a friend, or a family member. Dynasts give and/or volunteer mainly because it is part of their family tradition. No matter what the motivation, there is always one factor that stands out in the minds of the major donor. In his book *Megagifts*, Jerold Panas uncovers this factor, citing his research that proves donors give for many different reasons, but above all is the belief in the organization's mission.

Like donors, volunteers become involved for many reasons, including family history, religious influence, altruism, wanting to give back, community spirit, investing in their own or someone else's future, or because it is fun. But, if they do not believe in the mission of the organization, they will not be effective volunteers who can successfully ask a potential donor to contribute to the organization.

 TIPS & TECHNIQUES

Here are some cardinal rules of involving volunteers in fundraising that will be stressed throughout this book:

- Volunteers can only be effective if they truly believe in the mission of the organization.

- Volunteers should be invited to give of their time, talent, and treasure.

- Volunteers must be given meaningful work, not just busy work.

- Volunteers require staff support in order to be effective.

The mission is the driving force behind the organization's programs and activities—its reason for existence—and the mission needs to be clearly understood and accepted by the volunteers in order for them to be effective at fundraising for any organization.

Who is the ideal volunteer? "It is someone who is committed to your mission," says Betsy B. Clardy, CFRE, in *Advancing Philanthropy* (July/August 2004). "It is someone who has connections to people you cannot reach otherwise; someone who really wants to give of their time, talent and treasure to help you."

What motivates volunteers to get involved in an organization's fundraising efforts? For many Board members, fundraising is seen as an obligation to ensure the fiscal stability of the organization. For other volunteers, they may do so because (1) they have a connection to the organization—a relative who is a member of the staff or board; (2) they or a friend or relative have been recipients of the organization's services; or (3) they have been approached by another volunteer and invited to get involved. No matter what the motivation for getting involved, if they do not care about the cause, they will not be effective volunteers.

In a survey done by the author (*New Directions for Philanthropic Fundraising*), volunteers report that they are willing to do fundraising for those nonprofits that have a mission or cause in which they believe but also that give them the support volunteers need, including staff communication and information. Recognition gifts do not seem to excite volunteers, but a simple thank you, a published acknowledgment, or perhaps a fun recognition event is what they are looking for, according to the volunteers surveyed. Jim Ingolio's research on donor recognition can easily be transferred to recognition for volunteers. Ingolio found that "55 percent of all donors stop giving within the first year to a particular charity, and nearly 85 percent of all donors no longer give to the same charities by the fifth year after their first time gift."

The serious problem of donor attrition is often tied to acknowledgment and recognition of donors. Likewise, volunteer attrition often results when the nonprofit overlooks providing volunteers with the proper tools to enable them to succeed and fails to acknowledge their efforts. What types of recognition do donors and volunteers desire? Ingolio surveyed nonprofits and donors in Pennsylvania and found that although half the nonprofits surveyed said that donors display their tokens of appreciation, only one-third of the donors replied that they actually display those items. However, "80 percent of the donors felt that some form of recognition is important for good donor stewardship" and "only 20 percent of donors believed their charitable giving is motivated by recognition."

Likewise, volunteers agree that while they want to be recognized for their efforts, there does not have to be an elaborate gift or event for the organization to show appreciation for its volunteers. What is needed are (1) expectations that are clearly communicated, (2) the tools that will enable the volunteers to succeed, and (3) acknowledgment that the volunteer role is important to the organization. The importance of recognizing volunteers for their fundraising efforts, not only with token gifts, but by recognizing their contribution in a more personal way, is paramount to maintaining relationships with fundraising volunteers.

 IN THE REAL WORLD

Recognizing Volunteers

In a focus group, volunteers were asked how they felt about the organizations for which they volunteer, soliciting them for monetary contributions in addition to their volunteer time. There were varied responses to this question, but one points to the role of the importance of this intangible recognition of the volunteer efforts. One volunteer said he didn't mind being asked for a gift, but one organization he had volunteered for really made him angry when it sent him a direct mail piece, addressed to "Dear Friend," not recognizing his special relationship with the organization. He not only did not give to that appeal, but he also stopped volunteering for the organization.

According to the U.S. Bureau of Labor Statistics, more than 28 percent of all Americans volunteered in 2003. But how does the nonprofit get its "fair share" of these volunteers, and how does it find the volunteers who are willing to ask for money? Understanding what motivates volunteers can help in the recruitment process. Fundraising volunteers are a unique type of volunteer. Unfortunately, many people, even Board members, often say, "I'll do anything for this organization, but don't ask me to raise money. I can't ask anyone for money." So, how does an organization find those unique volunteers who actually enjoy asking for money? Or are these people a figment of the Development Director's imagination?

Is a Good Fundraiser Born or Is Fundraising an Acquired Skill?

Professional fundraisers often joke about the fact that no one sets out as a child to be a fundraiser when he or she grows up. Very few people appear to be "born to raise," although good fundraisers do seem to share some common traits. Panas lists qualities to look for in a professional fundraiser. The top five are (1) impeccable integrity, (2) good listener, (3) ability to motivate, (4) hard worker, and (5) concern for people.

These same qualities should be sought in volunteer fundraisers as well. Volunteer fundraisers certainly need to have integrity in order to gain the trust of potential donors. Volunteers will, at times, handle sensitive information about prospective donors such as prior giving history, relationship with the organization, and so on, and these volunteers must have a clear understanding of the ethical issues involved with their volunteer positions. People of integrity will be well respected in the community and can bring this respect and credibility to the organizations for which they volunteer.

Volunteer fundraisers must surely be good listeners. Eighty percent of communication with potential donors should be in listening, not in speaking.

Although volunteer fundraisers must be able to articulate the case, it is in listening that the volunteers will gain insight into the donors' needs and desires. Volunteers are often reluctant to accept the fundraising role because they think they are not the slick talker, salesperson type. These volunteers may not recognize that quiet, deep-thinking people are often more successful fundraisers because they listen to what the prospective donors are really saying and can often find the right hot button to prompt a major gift, simply because of this wonderful ability to listen. In fact, it is sometimes said that God gave us two ears and one mouth for a reason!

Volunteers, especially those who serve in leadership roles, must be able to inspire and motivate others to action. Because this quality is intangible, it sometimes takes trial and error to determine which volunteers truly have the ability to lead and inspire others. Usually they are people who are in leadership positions in their professions or leaders in their churches, synagogues, service clubs, and/or political arenas, but not always; it may be the person has never emerged as a community leader because he or she hasn't found a cause to feel passionate enough about to make it a major focus. The true leader possesses a special charisma. It is what Andy Stanley refers to in *Visioneering* when he says, "anybody who has ever received and followed through successfully with a God-given vision has possessed a form of authority that rests not on position or accomplishment, but on an inner conviction and the willingness to bring his or her life into alignment with that conviction." The nonprofit professional working with volunteers must always be on the lookout for those true visionary leaders who will surface from time to time, and cultivate these people to accept leadership roles within the organization where they will have the opportunity to inspire and motivate other volunteers to positive action.

There is no question that volunteering is hard work. Volunteer fundraisers must often be willing to learn new skills, to step out of their comfort zone, and to accept new responsibilities—and all of this is hard work. The time commitment alone is a lot of work for busy people. Many volunteers give so much of their time to a nonprofit that it is truly an avocation, and the best volunteers have enough free time to devote to the agreed-upon volunteer tasks. For this reason, entrepreneurs often make good volunteers because, while their time may be limited, a boss does not direct their schedule. However, if these people are passionate about the organization and its mission, they will find the time to be effective volunteers. Experience shows that those who really care about a cause will find the time to devote to it.

Finally, volunteer fundraisers must care about people. No matter the purpose of the fundraising—capital, endowment, or operating expenses—the truism of "people giving to people" should always be remembered. Volunteers who care about the people being served by the organization for which they volunteer will passionately communicate the case for support. Volunteer fundraisers must be sensitive to the needs of staff, other volunteers, the clients of the organization, and above all, the donors.

Fundraising can be taught and/or learned from experience. Today, courses for professional fundraisers are available online and on college campuses throughout North America. Although most of the participants in fundraising conferences, workshops, and formal education classes are professionals pursuing fundraising as a career, some volunteers will gladly avail themselves of this training in order to better help the organizations they care about. Particularly in grassroots organizations and in countries where fundraising is a fairly new profession, volunteers play a vital role in fundraising and are often the only fundraising support the organization has in its development efforts. These volunteers are often found at meetings, workshops, and conferences where they can learn more about fundraising in order to become more effective in their role as volunteer fundraisers.

Fundraising Roles for Volunteers

Most organizations rely heavily on volunteers when conducting a capital campaign, but often ignore the possibility of increasing their reach and effectiveness in

IN THE REAL WORLD

Volunteer Dedication

One consultant cites several instances of volunteers who, on their own time and money, have pursued ongoing education in the fundraising profession:

- One volunteer, who donated an enormous amount of her time for her children's preschool, attended a 10-month training program, at her own expense, in order to better help her organization with its fundraising efforts.

- When the Association of Fundraising Professionals' international conference was held in Philadelphia a few years ago, a married couple flew there from Phoenix, again at their own expense, because the wife was on the board of several nonprofits and wanted to enhance her ability to help these organizations with their fundraising.

- A volunteer fundraiser not only paid her own membership in the Association of Fundraising Professionals and attended all of the meetings and conferences held by her chapter at her own expense, but also served on the Board of the chapter.

fundraising by using volunteers throughout all of their fundraising efforts. Numerous fundraising activities can effectively use volunteers, including the following:

- Special events.
- Annual fund.
    - Direct mail.
    - Telephone fundraising.
    - Corporate appeals.

- Grant proposals.
- Major gifts appeals.
- Capital and endowment campaigns.
- Planned giving efforts.

Some of these activities are traditionally known to be volunteer dependent, but all of them can effectively use volunteers. Greenfield says, "Every activity has an absolute need for volunteer leadership. Without someone to recruit others, conduct the meetings, provide direction (and respect), keep the program on track, and insist on performance and success, the entire effort is lost." Although staff can certainly fill many, if not all, of these roles, volunteer leadership brings a new dimension to these fundraising activities by providing that essential ingredient—an outside perspective that looks at the organization and the task at hand as a special avocation. The following chapters discuss in detail these various roles volunteers can play in a nonprofit organization's fundraising efforts.

Why Volunteers Are Effective at Making the Ask

"Leadership Volunteers have the ability to influence retention and the upward movement of donors more than anyone else" (Burk). Volunteers are in a unique position to ask others for money for several reasons: (1) They aren't getting paid to do it; (2) They have a real commitment to the mission of the organization; (3) They have already made a significant contribution themselves; (4) They care enough that they are taking time from their "real work" to participate in the non-profit organization's fundraising program; and (5) They are often doing a task that they don't really savor, but for which they recognize a need. Few people actual-ly enjoy asking others for money. Although many volunteers out there are really good at it, most of them will say they really don't enjoy it. So, if they are willing to do something they don't really enjoy without any pay, some other reward must keep them coming back and make them successful at what they do.

Kay Sprinkel Grace says, "Volunteer involvement is a basic component of the nonprofit sector's capacity to respond to community needs." Without volunteer fundraisers, many organizations would need to hire huge development staffs, driving up the cost of fundraising and forcing the organizations to cut back on the very reason for their existence—program! Grace goes on to say, "Because volunteers represent the community, they provide insight and perspective that nonprofits must have to shape their programs and outreach appropriately."

One of the reasons why volunteers are so good at asking for money is simply that they are *volunteers*. This does not mean to say that staff people are not committed to their organizations. Many readers will be able to cite numerous instances of staff people (perhaps themselves) who have been with their organization for many years and are obviously committed to the organization. Let's face it, most people do not work for a nonprofit because of the huge salary they are pulling down, but rather because they believe in what the organization is doing. The recent trend toward more stability in the profession points out the fact that development officers are staying in their jobs longer because of this commitment, but there is still that special commitment that comes only with volunteering. In fact, most development staff people still volunteer for some other nonprofits in their free time—at their church, their children's school, the local Chamber of Commerce, the AFP or another professional organization, or some other agency whose mission is especially close to their hearts. As volunteers themselves, most development people will understand that special feeling that comes from volunteering that is different from the satisfaction received on the job.

Another reason why volunteers can be more effective than staff is that they are generally soliciting their peers and approaching people to give at a level at which they themselves have already given. For this reason, it is recommended that staff and volunteers call on major donors as a team. (More about this topic in a later chapter.) Volunteers can easily tell peers that they have already made an investment in this organization themselves because they believe so strongly in the good work the organization is doing. They can then invite prospective donors to join them in this investment. Greenfield says that when a solicitation comes from a friend, "the information and intent are trusted," and the enthusiasm of the volunteer can be the convincing factor to persuade the donors to give.

The volunteer role in fundraising is critical because of the sincerity and commitment volunteers bring to the table, the connections that often would not be available to the nonprofit fundraiser, and the special expertise and leadership qualities that lend credibility to the organization.

Summary

Volunteers are the foundation of a strong development program. Although this is accepted as part of the definition of philanthropy, most organizations underuse volunteers or use them in the wrong ways. Among the ways volunteers can play a meaningful role in the organization's development program are the following:

- Special events.
- Annual fund.
  - Direct mail.
  - Telephone fundraising.
  - Business appeals.
- Grant proposals.
- Major gift efforts.
- Capital campaigns.
- Planned giving.

Although the fundraising program must be a joint effort between staff and volunteers, volunteers are generally more effective at fundraising than staff for several reasons:

- They are volunteers, not in paid staff positions.
- They believe strongly in the mission of the organization.

- They have already made a financial commitment at the level at which they are asking the prospects to give.

- They are asking peers to join them in investing in the organization.

Further Reading

Boice, Jacklyn. *Advancing Philanthropy*. Alexandria, VA: Association of Fundraising Professionals, July/August 2004.

Burk, Penelope. *Donor-Centered Fundraising, U.S. Edition*. Chicago: Burk & Associates, 2003.

Grace, Kay Sprinkel. *Beyond Fundraising*. New York: John Wiley & Sons, 1997.

Greenfield, James. *Fundraising*, 2nd ed. New York: John Wiley & Sons, 1999.

Gurin, Maurice. *Advancing Beyond the Techniques of Fundraising*. Rockville, MD: Taft Group, 1991.

Ingolio, James B. "Donor Affirmation." *Ventures in Philanthropy*. Reading, PA: Capital Venture, Spring 2004.

Lysakowski, Linda. "What's in It for Me?" *New Directions in Philanthropy*. San Francisco: Jossey-Bass, 2003.

Nichols, Judith. *Pinpointing Affluence*. Chicago: Precept Press, 1994.

Panas, Jerold. *Born to Raise*. Chicago: Pluribus Press, 1988.

Panas, Jerold. *Megagifts*. Chicago: Pluribus Press, 1984.

Prince, Russ Alan, and Karen Maru File. *The Seven Faces of Philanthropy*. San Francisco: Jossey-Bass, 1995.

Stanley, Andy. *Visioneering*. Sisters, OR: Multnomah, 1999.

CHAPTER 2

Finding and Recruiting Fundraising Volunteers

After reading this chapter, you will be able to:

- List sources of potential fundraising volunteers.
- List techniques to be used in matching volunteers with fundraising tasks.
- List the steps necessary for volunteer recruitment.

Finding Volunteer Fundraisers

With the Why of using volunteers answered, it is time to look at Who recruits volunteers, and How, Where, and When they are recruited. Where does one start when looking for volunteer fundraisers? Volunteers, like major donors, usually don't drop from the sky. The volunteer recruitment process is the first step in building a team of volunteer fundraisers for any organization.

The education and training, management, and recognition processes are covered in later chapters. For now, let's focus on where to find volunteer fundraisers and how to recruit them. First, a profile of the volunteer fundraisers needed

TIPS & TECHNIQUES

The recruitment process includes:

- Developing a profile of the volunteers the organization needs.

- Developing a list of potential volunteers.

- Finding the right person to make the ask.

- Welcoming and orienting the volunteers.

- Providing education and support for the volunteers.

- Managing the volunteer program.

- Appreciating and recognizing volunteers.

should be developed. It is important to understand the qualities expected to be found in good fundraisers, what the volunteers will expect of the organization, and the expectations the organization has of the volunteers. Only then can appropriate volunteer position descriptions be developed.

Qualities of Volunteer Fundraisers

Integrity and passion for the mission were discussed in Chapter 1, but it cannot be said too often that these two critical elements are needed in order for volunteers to be successful at fundraising. Although integrity may seem to be an intangible quality and one that is difficult to define in clear terms, people of integrity are generally recognized in their communities as those of character, who deal fairly in their business and personal relationships. Another way to look at it is that people of integrity can relate well to people in all walks of life. In fundraising, this ability is important because the potential donor may be a high-profile person with an

TIPS & TECHNIQUES

Good volunteer fundraisers have the following qualities:

- Integrity.

- Passion for the organization's mission.

- Ability to maintain strict confidence of donor and organization information.

- Excellent communication skills.

- Contacts with major donors.

- Ability to work as part of a team.

important position, but could just as easily be a down-to-earth millionaire next door, the person who wears an off-the-rack suit, drives a beat-up old station wagon, and runs an unglamorous business such as pest control or paving. True people of integrity are able to relate with the CEO as well as the janitor of any company—and either one could be a major donor for an organization.

Volunteers perform better when they really care about the mission of an organization, but it is critical that fundraising volunteers have this fire in the belly. Asking for money is a sensitive issue, and unless volunteers are really committed to the organization, they will find reasons not to make a fundraising call. When the volunteers have that passion for the organization's mission, it is a delight and a pleasure for them to invite others to join them in investing in the organization.

Also crucial to fundraising volunteers is the ability to maintain confidence of the things that are discussed within the fundraising operation. Sensitive information about prospective donors is often shared with fundraising volunteers, and these volunteers must understand the importance of maintaining the confidentiality of these sensitive items. Also, during their relationship with other volunteers in the fundraising program, they may become privy to sensitive information about these volunteers and/or their companies and need to maintain a professional approach to this information. It is also vital that the nonprofit share information about its operations with volunteers when that information will be necessary to help them answer questions from potential donors. Therefore, the organization will want to ensure that the volunteers show good judgment about what information they share, when, and with whom.

Fundraising volunteers need to have good communication skills, both written and verbal. It is essential for volunteers to be able to communicate with the organization, other volunteers, and prospective donors. Today, many organizations communicate with their volunteers through e-mail, so volunteers who are Internet-savvy are a real plus for the organization. Also, fundraising volunteers are often asked to write letters, articles for newsletters, and other printed fundraising tools, so having good writing ability is essential. Although in most cases the staff does the writing and asks the volunteers to endorse it or make it more personal, some volunteers prefer writing their own letters and having them approved and mailed by staff. Fundraising volunteers should *never* send out any communications without the knowledge of the staff. Volunteers who will be involved in thank-a-thons, phone-a-thons, or any other telephone program need to have good telephone communication skills. Phone-a-thon volunteers are often recruited from those in careers where they have had training in telephone skills—realtors, financial planners, insurance salespeople, stock brokers, call center personnel, and people from other sales industries where telephone prospecting is prevalent make good volunteers for telephone fundraising programs. However, because most major fundraising is done face-to-face, it is most important that fundraising volunteers have a good ability to communicate one-on-one with potential donors. Especially in the case of volunteer leadership, there will often be occasions for fundraising volunteers to make group presentations, so a good stage presence is needed.

Volunteers with contacts in the community make the best fundraising volunteers. Because most volunteers feel more comfortable asking people they know, the volunteer needs to be a person who knows and can get an appointment with the prospective donor. Often people in the same fields as those suggested for telephone fundraising have a lot of contacts in the community (e.g., realtors, insurance people, bankers). When looking for planned gifts, estate planners, attorneys, and trust officers generally have contacts with prospective planned giving donors. However, the nonprofit needs to be careful not to make the mistake that many development people make—thinking that the quiet, unassuming person has no contacts in the community. People who appear to lead ordinary lives may have contacts with some amazing prospective donors through their houses of worship, professional associations, or service clubs. Careful volunteer development will take advantage of these situations that can be helpful to the organization.

Volunteers who have the ability to work as a team are essential for the nonprofit. Most successful major gift calls involve two or more people teaming up to make a presentation to the prospective donor(s). The volunteers need to work closely with other volunteers and staff to achieve success. Teamwork is discussed more in a future chapter, but it is important to look for this quality when recruiting volunteers. Volunteers who seem more concerned about how their involvement with the organization will benefit them are likely not to be good team players and may not keep the interests of the donors and the organization above their own interests. Volunteers who want to bask in the glory of their accomplishments are not as effective as those who truly care about the organization and the donors and want to bring the two together, in what Doug Lawson calls the art of fundraising through the bringing together of "a joyful donor, a grateful recipient, and an artful asker."

Don't forget, however, that the volunteers have expectations about the volunteer experience, just as the organization has expectations of the volunteers. Most volunteers have a list of things they look for when presented with different volunteer opportunities. The organization that meets their criteria will be the one they volunteer for and the one for which they will do a good job. In *Advancing Philanthropy* (July/August 2004), David Biegler, Outstanding Volunteer Fundraiser for 2003, says, "It has to be something that I feel passionately about. You're only as good as your passion leads you to be. If you don't care or if you don't volunteer for the right reasons, it is just a job and you'll get tired of it." Ann Bedsole, the 2004 recipient of the Outstanding Volunteer Fundraiser award, adds that there is something in the challenging task that excites her. "I don't support things that would be easy for someone else to do. If it's some project that everybody loves, there's no point working on that. Anyone can raise the money. Other things are harder to raise money for, and you have to help meet their needs to have a healthy community."

In a survey done by the author, volunteers in general say their number-one expectation of the volunteer experience is that the organization will use their time and talents wisely, with female respondents giving a higher priority to the wise use of their time. Second in ranking of expectations were that the volunteers would receive a position description or some listing of the expectations of the volunteers. The organization that is prepared to meet volunteers' expectations will be most successful at recruiting and retaining volunteer fundraisers.

Sometimes volunteers will find the agency that is just right for them, whereas other times the agency will need to seek out the volunteers. People who have a connection to the organization, such as alumni; relatives or friends of staff members, Board members, or clients; or people who do business with the organization, may have heard good things about the organization and want to get involved. Volunteers may come to an organization through their affiliation with a church or professional association or they may have been referred by a volunteer center, but more often, the organization needs to take a proactive role in the recruitment of volunteers. Therefore, the development staff will need to work with the chief executive officer, Board members, and other volunteers to find the right volunteers for the job at hand. Staff members who are good at networking have the best chance of finding appropriate volunteers for the work to be done. Development officers should make connections with business, service, and professional clubs and social contacts outside of the nonprofit arena. Nonprofit staff members are often so busy networking with others in their field that they forget to make those important connections outside of their immediate comfort zone.

Where to Find Volunteers

How does an organization begin to find fundraising volunteers? For some organizations that have been using volunteers in other areas, such as program or administrative areas, a good suggestion is to start with those volunteers who already have expressed an interest in and commitment to the organization. Bringing these volunteers together for a meeting to explain the fundraising area of the organization and discussing the fundraising roles for which the organization is looking to recruit volunteers is one place to start. Another option is to survey current volunteers to see which ones have an interest in taking on new responsibilities in the form of fundraising roles. Many organizations have used volunteers in minor fundraising roles, such as special events or mail stuffing. Perhaps these volunteers have other skills and talents and an interest in becoming involved at a higher level. Again, these volunteers can be asked individually or as a group to step up to a higher level of involvement.

For organizations that have never used volunteers, it may be a little more challenging, but a good place to start is with those who have already shown an interest in the organization or have a tie to it. Alumni are found in many organizations, not just schools, colleges, and universities. Perhaps the organization has people who have gone through a rehab program, taken an art class, been a blood donor, and so on. These are the organization alumni, and they should not be overlooked. They already know the organization and are often committed to it.

One Organization's Unique Alumni

A Golden Retriever rescue group in the midst of a capital campaign held a phone-a-thon, in which volunteers who had adopted a Golden Retriever in the year 1995, for example, called other alumni who had also adopted dogs that year to compare notes on their Goldens and ask for a pledge to the capital campaign. It was a great way for the adopters to connect with other folks sharing a similar experience and was a successful way to raise money for a new facility.

There are other ways to attract fundraising volunteers. Local Chambers of Commerce are great ways to connect with business people and entrepreneurs, who are often looking for ways to get more involved in their communities. Many communities also have leadership programs, in which midlevel managers enroll in a year–long program to learn more about their communities and the nonprofit world, with the ultimate goal of serving on the board of a nonprofit organization. These leadership programs can be a great source of volunteers. Most nonprofit leaders are accustomed to the "rubber chicken circuit," speaking at meetings and gatherings of local service and professional associations that might be able to volunteer as a group or individually for the organization. Many communities also have a volunteer center, which matches volunteers with organizations and does a lot of the screening in advance so the organization does not need to do that.

Past donors are an especially good source of volunteers. If they have supported the organization already, it will be easy for them to invite others to join them in this investment. A group of past donors could be invited to a special luncheon at which time volunteer opportunities are presented.

Another way to find good volunteers is to involve staff and board members in the identification process. A grid similar to the one shown in Exhibit 4.1 for identifying donors for the organization can be developed to focus on volunteer needs. Have Board and staff members brainstorm at a meeting to identify a list of potential volunteers and then develop a plan to select those who meet the needs of the organization for volunteers and develop a plan for recruiting these volunteers.

 TIPS & TECHNIQUES

Sources of Volunteers

- Donors.
- Other volunteers.
- Clients or users of services.
- Service clubs (e.g., Rotary, Lions, Sertoma, Kiwanis).
- Churches and religious institutions.
- Chambers of Commerce.
- Board members' suggestions.
- Development Committee suggestions.
- Planning study interviewees' suggestions (if a planning study has been done).
- Website.
- Newsletter.
- Staff contacts.
- Networking.

Development officers need to get involved with their local Chamber of Commerce and other professional and service clubs. Don't just join—get involved! If the organization is conducting a capital campaign, a planning study (or feasibility study) is generally done beforehand to determine the level of support

IN THE REAL WORLD

Time, Talent, and Treasure

One organization introduced its brand-new Development Department to the full staff (more than 200 people in three divisions of the organization) by holding a Time, Talent, and Treasure Hunt. A treasure chest was filled with "jewels" and gold-wrapped chocolate candy coins. Sprinkled among the treasures were some prizes (e.g., gift certificates to local restaurants, beauty shops). The Development Director and Chair of the Development Committee each made a brief presentation at all three divisional staff meetings so the entire staff would hear the presentation. The Development Director explained the role of the Development Office and how it would work within the organization. The Chair of the Development Committee explained that although the Development Office was instituted to help the organization raise money, fundraising was really everyone in the organization's job, and that the Development Office needed the help of the staff. Several options were presented by which staff members could help with their gifts of time, talent, and treasure. Each staff person received a card on which they could list their name and the ways they could help the Development Office. Cards were collected at each staff meeting, and prizes were drawn at random for those who had filled out a card. The results were amazing. Staff members suggested friends and relatives who could serve on the Development Committee, possible donors, and offered a variety of talents such as doing calligraphy on invitations, providing music for an event, and offering their time to work at events or help with telephoning.

that can be expected. One of the important questions that the consultant will ask during this process is whether the interviewees would be interested in becoming involved as volunteers in this campaign or whether they have any recommendations for campaign leadership. Be sure to follow up on these responses once the campaign volunteer recruitment process begins. Do some brainstorming with current volunteers and donors; invite them to an informational meeting where the various volunteer opportunities are presented. Ask Board members and staff to recommend friends and relatives who might be interested in volunteering for the organization.

Determining the volunteer requirements will be different for every organization. One organization may be contemplating a capital campaign and will need to put a solid campaign volunteer structure in place. Another may be trying to expand the role of volunteers in its annual fund, while another is preparing to recruit volunteers for a Development Committee or Planned Giving Council. In Chapter 3, these various roles are discussed in detail, along with the skills and talents required by different fundraising volunteers. The next logical step is to develop a list of position descriptions to fit the volunteer needs of the organization.

Position descriptions should be clear about the overall responsibilities, the specific tasks assigned to volunteers, the reporting structure, and the time commitment involved. See Exhibit 3.2 for several sample position descriptions that can be adapted by an organization to suit its particular needs.

Recruiting Volunteers

Staff, Board members, or other volunteers can recruit volunteers other than Board members. Volunteers are often the best choice to involve other volunteers. Getting the volunteers involved in finding people like themselves who share an interest in the organization's mission is the best way to recruit additional volunteers.

As with engaging donors, much can be learned from Henry Rosso's concentric circle theory. Start enlisting the donors who will be closest to the project first, the chairs or co-chairs, and then, from the inner circle, spread outward to involve as many volunteers as possible in the fundraising effort. People tend to give more once they are engaged and involved in the project, so more volunteers will generally mean more dollars for your program.

Once volunteers are engaged, they need to be welcomed into the organization just as Board members receive an orientation. Jim Greenfield recommends that those who accept volunteer positions within the organization should receive an official welcome letter from the senior volunteer or Board member who was responsible for recruiting them. Greenfield says this welcome letter should include "details about the assignment, its importance to the organization, the goal, and the term of office" of the volunteer assignment. A volunteer orientation session should also be scheduled for volunteers working on the same project, whether it is a capital campaign, the annual fund, or a planned giving program. Volunteers want to see that others are engaged in the program and that they are not in it alone. Volunteers also like to network with their peers, so the orientation session is a good opportunity for them to get to know each other as well as learn more about the organization. If possible at such an orientation session, have a recipient of the organization's programs speak. This is a great motivational tool and helps involve volunteers directly in the organization's mission.

The leadership of the organization, both the chief executive and the chair of the Board, must be present to welcome volunteers, especially those who will be involved in high-level asks. Materials can be given out at this time about the organization in general, things like an annual report, a brochure or CD, a list of Board members and staff, and the organization's strategic plan. A visual overview of the organization's structure can also be made through a video or PowerPoint presentation. Provide an opportunity for feedback from the volunteers. Most people love giving their opinions and will feel involved in the organization if they are invited to give input into the plans and vision of the organization.

IN THE REAL WORLD

Volunteer Orientation

A college held an annual orientation session for its annual fund volunteers. During this orientation, a student on scholarship spoke about how important the scholarship was to her and a faculty member explained a new program the college was offering. The College President welcomed volunteers and the Volunteer Chair gave a motivational talk about why he was involved in the college's annual drive, even though he had no direct connection to this school. Each volunteer was given a notebook containing the case for support, annual fund brochures, an annual report, and an outline of the training program conducted by the Vice President for Development. Along with these materials, each volunteer received the pledge cards for the prospects assigned to them, a list of their assignments with information about each prospect garnered through research and prior giving history, and their own pledge card.

Summary

People volunteer for various reasons, but primarily because they have a passion for the mission of the organizations for which they volunteer. Sometimes volunteers will seek out a nonprofit for which they want to volunteer, but most often nonprofits need to be proactive in the volunteer recruitment process. Development staff people need to network into the many different areas in which volunteers can be found.

Further Reading

Boice, Jacklyn. *Advancing Philanthropy*. Alexandria, VA: July/August 2004.

Greenfield, James. *Fundraising*, 2nd ed. New York: John Wiley & Sons, 1999.

Lawson, Douglas M. *Give to Live*. San Diego, CA: ALTI Publishing, 1991.

Lysakowski, Linda. "Volunteers in the Twenty-first Century." Unpublished study, funded through the Associations of Fundraising Professionals Research Council, Alexandria, VA, 1999.

Stanley, Thomas, and William Danko. *The Millionaire Next Door*. New York: Pocket Books (Simon & Schuster), 1998.

CHAPTER 3

Volunteer Positions in the Capital Campaign

 After reading this chapter, you will be able to:

- Define the role of volunteers in a capital campaign.
- Describe the ideal campaign chair.
- Develop position descriptions for capital campaign positions.

The Importance of Volunteers in the Capital Campaign

Because capital campaigning is one of the best examples of the use of volunteer fundraisers and because much of what is learned in recruiting volunteers for capital campaigns can be translated into other areas of fundraising, this important volunteer function will be discussed first.

Most organizations will be faced at one time or another with planning a major effort to raise money for capital expenditures—a new building, renovations to an existing facility, major equipment purchases, or building their endowment.

In order to accomplish this task, a capital campaign is usually the direction these organizations follow. One of the major differences between capital campaigning and other fundraising efforts for many organizations is the number and the caliber of volunteers that are used.

In *Getting Ready for a Capital Campaign*, Lysakowski and Snyder outline some of the steps taken early in a campaign to assess the quality and quantity of volunteers that will be available to help with the campaign. As part of the internal assessment of campaign readiness, consultants generally will look at the role the Board has played in fundraising, the strength of the Development Committee or Development Council, and whether the organization has utilized volunteers in its annual fundraising effort. Determining the availability of volunteer leadership is one of the most important factors in assessing the potential for a successful campaign. The planning study (sometimes called the feasibility study) done in preparation for a campaign is invaluable in identifying and cultivating potential campaign volunteers. During the study, consultants ask interviewees about their willingness to accept a leadership or other volunteer role in the campaign. Interviewees are also asked to identify other potential volunteers who might have an interest in the organization and in this campaign. If volunteers are not available, the consultants will often recommend delaying the campaign until such

 TIPS & TECHNIQUES

Steps to Recruiting Compaign Volunteers

- Recruit the Steering Committee.
- Recruit the Campaign Chairs.
- Recruit the Campaign Cabinet (Committee Chairs).
- Guide the Committee Chairs in recruiting their committees.

time as committed, talented volunteers are available to serve in leadership roles in the campaign.

Capital and endowment campaigns generally rely heavily on volunteers to be effective. As in a major gifts appeal, discussed in Chapter 4, volunteers are involved in identifying, cultivating, and soliciting donors. Most capital campaigns involve hundreds of volunteers in their effort to raise the significant dollars that are needed. Although this task sounds daunting, especially to the organization that has not previously involved volunteers as fundraisers, it can be accomplished by following a carefully planned process.

By following this process, a capital campaign can effectively use volunteers to plan the campaign and identify, cultivate, and solicit donors, with a minimal amount of stress for the staff. Remember that as Kent Dove says, "All volunteers are not equal!" Recruiting the right volunteers for the job is more important than the number of volunteers involved. In *Good to Great*, Jim Collins talks about getting the "right people on the bus, and in the right seats." Collins asserts that first we must decide who and then what. Having the right people on the bus will ensure that the campaign is successful, no matter what changes take place in the organization, the campaign goals, the staff, and the environment. In his earlier book, *Built to Last*, Collins studied companies in similar industries to see what made the difference in those that achieved great success and those that settled for mediocrity or fell into oblivion. If Collins had studied nonprofit organizations, this author's contention is that the results would be similar—those that achieve greatness start with determining "first who, then what."

For nonprofits this challenge may be even more difficult than it is for businesses. After all, the only group of players that the company generally needs to recruit is its employees. The nonprofit, however, has staff, Board, and volunteers that it must carefully choose and put into the right seats on the bus. So, how does a nonprofit ensure that the right volunteers are on board and are doing the right tasks? By starting with the first group in the circle of volunteers and working its way to the outer circle.

Rosso's Concentric Circles

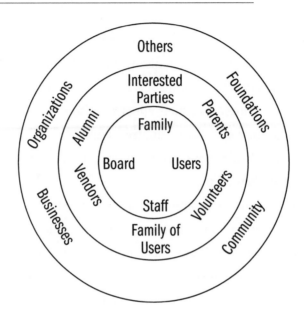

The Role of the Board in a Capital Campaign

Kent Dove says, "The chair of the board, the chair of the campaign and the chief executive officer of the organization have the principle roles in a capital campaign. The success or failure of most campaigns is ultimately attributable to them." The Board members' role is perhaps the single most critical factor in the campaign's success. The Board will guide the project, determine the goal of the campaign, recruit volunteers for the campaign cabinet, and be an integral part of identifying, cultivating, and soliciting major gifts for the campaign. The Board must fully support the project and the campaign and should pass a resolution at a Board meeting to initiate a campaign. Several Board members must step up to the plate and be willing to serve in leadership roles during the campaign. All Board members must financially support the campaign, and all should be involved in identifying, cultivating, and soliciting donors, as well as promoting the campaign publicly. Without buy-in from the Board, no campaign can succeed.

A capital campaign must be top priority for the Board and staff before an organization can expect volunteers to jump on the bandwagon.

The Steering Committee

In a capital campaign, another key part of this inner circle is the Steering Committee. The Steering Committee is a fairly small number of people, usually not more than seven, who guide the precampaign process and select the Campaign Cabinet. Steering Committee members are involved in the early planning process in preparation for the campaign during the period when the organization is doing strategic planning, architectural planning, the internal assessment of the organization, and the external analysis of the community's readiness. Steering Committee members must be carefully chosen from a pool of people who possess the skills to do this early planning.

 TIPS & TECHNIQUES

Some of the attributes needed by the Steering Committee include the following:

- Ability to think logically and clearly in order to develop appropriate plans and timelines.

- Financial knowledge in order to understand budgeting for the project and the campaign.

- Knowledge of facilities and construction.

- Commitment to the long-term vision of the organization.

- Knowledge of the external environment of the organization, especially the philanthropic community.

IN THE REAL WORLD

The Steering Committee

One organization selected a Steering Committee, calling them the A-Team, who had the skills and talents that uniquely qualified them to serve as part of this elite group. The Campaign Chair was a senior program officer at a leading foundation in the community, who also chaired the Steering Committee. His foundation was not a potential donor for the organization because of the restrictions this foundation had on its giving program; however, his ability to understand the philanthropic environment in that community was invaluable, along with his commitment to both the organization and the project. His knowledge of building and planning proved essential to the campaign success. Along with the Campaign Chair, the A-Team included the Campaign Consultants, the Chief Executive Officer of the organization, the Chief Financial Officer of the organization, the PR/media relations person (this organization had no development staff per se), and the Campaign Coordinator (a staff person moved to this position temporarily for the duration of the campaign). This A-Team met twice a month initially, and then later monthly, between the Campaign Cabinet meetings, to establish the agenda for cabinet meetings, review the budget and timeline, discuss recruitment and replacement of cabinet members as needed, and monitor building and campaign progress.

Steering Committee members generally include both staff and volunteers. Staff members who should be a part of the Steering Committee include the Chief Executive Officer, the Chief Development Officer, the Chief Financial Officer, and a Facilities Manager, if there is one on staff. If there is no one on the staff with knowledge of facilities, finance, or development, these roles will be filled by volunteers; therefore, it is vital to seek people with knowledge in the areas lacking by staff. The Board Chair is usually part of the Steering Committee, along with Board members who have expertise needed by this committee.

The Chair of the Finance Committee, Chair of the Development Committee, or others with specialized knowledge can guide the organization during this crucial planning phase. If a major donor for the project has been identified, it is wise to include that person in the planning process by making her or him a part of the Steering Committee. Donors who are also involved as volunteers early in the process will be able to help identify and recruit other donors and volunteers.

The Campaign Chair(s)

The Campaign Chair is the visible leader of the effort to raise significant dollars, and it is essential to have a person or persons who are well known and respected in the community to head this effort. Often co-chairs, and sometimes even an Office of the Chair is used, whereby several people share the chair role, sometimes each for a period of time, then turning over the reins to another member of the office. Finding the right chair(s) is critical to the success of the campaign. The right person heading the campaign can often deliver dollars and volunteers that the organization might never have imagined would be supportive of the project. Choosing the right chair must be a well-thought-out process. Start by outlining the expectations and requirements of a chair, developing the position description, and then making a list of potential candidates for chairpersonship. Determine the number of people needed to fulfill the leadership role: a single chair, an honorary chair and a general chair, co-chairs, or multiple chairs as in the office of the chair model. Keep in mind that the chair will need visionary leadership abilities, have the ability to make a significant gift to the campaign, and be capable of inspiring and motivating other volunteers. Sometimes an Honorary Chair is appointed, particularly when organizations feel the need to add credibility to their campaigns by involving a high-profile person who may not have the time or energy to devote to serving in an active role on the Campaign Cabinet, but whose standing in the community would enhance the public image of the organization and the campaigns.

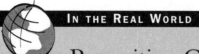

Recruiting Campaign Leadership

A group of volunteer firefighters who had never run a capital campaign found themselves in need of making major renovations to their fire training school. Although the Board was fairly large (33 members) and committed to the organization, they were not people of affluence or influence in their community. Recognizing the need to involve some key community players, they (along with their consultant) developed a plan to approach the CEO of the largest business in their community and ask him to serve as the Honorary Chair of the campaign, believing he would not have the time to attend meetings and get heavily involved in the campaign solicitations. They put together a recruitment packet that included the case for support, the campaign timeline, and the position description for the honorary campaign chair.

The prospective Honorary Chair met with the chair of the Board, another Board member, and the campaign consultant. As the plan was laid out to the prospective volunteer, he became interested in the project and had just one question. When seeing the position description requirement of making a significant gift, he asked what dollar amount that was. Pointing to the top giving level, the team suggested that they would like him to consider a gift at that level.

The volunteer not only said he would accept the Honorary Chair position, but he actually attended every Campaign Cabinet meeting, gave a major gift, and signed a letter inviting other volunteers to join him in this effort. Because they were successful in enlisting this high-profile community leader, the organization was able to recruit top management from every local bank and numerous other business and community leaders to serve on its Campaign Cabinet.

In most cases, the co-chair or office of the chair model is recommended for several reasons. First, having two or more chairs immediately lessens the workload on the volunteers. Also, just as in team solicitations for gifts, having two

The Office of the Chair

A private school held a capital campaign with three people serving in the Office of the Chair. Two of these people were major donors to the campaign, and all three had been involved in the Steering Committee, which had worked for several years to plan the project and the campaign. One of the major donors was a successful business leader who did not have a lot of time to devote to the campaign but was willing to lend his name, along with making one of the two lead gifts to the campaign. The giver of the other lead gift was able to attend campaign meetings and agreed to make a limited number of major gift asks but was reluctant to preside over meetings. The third member of the team, although not able to contribute financially at the same level as the other two co-chairs, made a gift that was significant, agreed to preside at meetings, and gave countless hours of his time to identify, cultivate, and solicit donors. This triumvirate proved to be the ideal team for this project, because they had all been parents of students at the school, each gave at a stretch level for their individual situations, and they brought the ideal mix of talents and abilities to lead.

people each bringing their own unique perspective and talents to bear on the task at hand can be effective. There may also be value in recruiting people representing more than one gender, ethnicity, age, geographic area, or constituency representation. For example, a school may want to have an alumnus/alumna and a local business leader co-chair its campaign; a hospital may want to have a medical professional and a nonmedical community leader co-chair. For some organizations, a husband and wife team or a team of significant others make a logical choice to chair a campaign effort.

The Campaign Chair(s) needs to be selected carefully. The person(s) selected must be a proven leader(s), able to inspire greatness in others, willing to devote his or her time, capable of and willing to make a significant gift to the campaign, committed to the mission and vision of the organization, and free from any thoughts of personal gain through affiliation with the campaign or the organization. A sample position description for a Campaign Chair is included in Exhibit 3.2 at the end of this chapter.

Campaign Cabinet

The Campaign Cabinet is the group of people responsible for all aspects of the capital campaign, from planning to implementation; approving policies and budgets for the campaign; identifying, cultivating, and soliciting donors; and planning campaign events and publicity. Recruitment of the Campaign Cabinet should start with the Chair(s), as outlined previously, and then, with the help of the Chair(s), the rest of the cabinet members should be carefully selected, again according to the skills and talents needed to fulfill the tasks for each position. The campaign plan should outline all positions that will be needed, along with the position description for each volunteer position. Like the Campaign Chair(s), the cabinet members must have certain qualities. Before recruiting any campaign volunteers, it is crucial to first have a campaign plan that includes an organizational chart outlining the divisions of the campaign and the volunteers that will head each division and position descriptions for each of these volunteers. A sample organizational chart is included at the end of this chapter (Exhibit 3.1), along with sample position descriptions (Exhibit 3.2).

The Campaign Cabinet will comprise the chairs of each division. Although each campaign will have different divisions according to the organization's needs, all campaigns will need these tasks filled—committees to identify, cultivate, and solicit donors at various levels; a publicity committee; a special events committee; and committees to reach out to each of the organization's constituencies. It is vital to recruit the right volunteers and assign them to the right positions. Just as an organization would not hire a staff person and then find a job for that person to

Creating Campaign Divisions

One organization embarking on a capital campaign had developed a Campaign Cabinet based on the divisions that were identified by the consultant and leadership of the organization. As volunteer recruiting began, it became clear that because this was a statewide organization in a fairly large state, it was going to be challenging to fill all of the Campaign Cabinet seats with people who could reach all of the organization's constituents with ease. A cabinet position was filled for each division, but then under many of these divisions (all those involved in direct solicitation), four vice chairs were recruited, one for each area of the state, to coordinate efforts in their region. The regional vice chairs were only responsible for their geographic area and worked closely with the other divisions' regional vice chairs from their areas. Four separate kickoff events were also planned, so the Special Events Chair also recruited four regional vice chairs. Thus, all of the divisions had one (or two when co-chairs were used) clear leader, and this leader(s) was able to cover all of the areas of the state through the regional vice chairs.

do, it should never recruit campaign volunteers without knowing clearly in advance what that person brings to the campaign and what is expected from this person. For example, if there is a small business division in the campaign, it is critical to involve a large number of volunteers from small and medium–sized businesses that have connections and clout with other business leaders.

When soliciting lead and major donors, it is necessary to have volunteers who have made significant gifts of their own serve on this committee, in order to have them ask others for gifts at these levels. A special events chair is needed to plan and implement the various events (not fundraising events) that are an important part of a campaign (e.g., kickoff events, groundbreaking, dedication events, and victory celebrations). The special event volunteer chair(s) must be well organized and detail oriented. Public relations chairs need to be recruited who have skills and talents in graphic design, access to printing companies, media contacts, and other talents that are needed to effectively promote the campaign. Although each organization's needs for Campaign Cabinet members is different, there must always be a strong corps of volunteers willing to accomplish the task of fundraising for the campaign.

Committee Members

Once the Campaign Cabinet is in place, each Committee Chair or Chairs will recruit their own committee members. People asking people they know is how most volunteers get recruited. It is helpful, however, in this process for the organization to have a list of potential volunteers—names gathered during the planning study, volunteers who are already involved in the organization's fundraising efforts, and people identified by the Campaign Cabinet and committee chairs to be involved. One good source of identifying potential volunteers needed for each committee involved in the solicitation process is to develop a preliminary prospect list for that division and then contact those who are expected to give at a certain level, seeking to involve them as volunteers first, before asking for their donation. People are far more likely to make generous gifts to the campaign if they are serving on a committee for the campaign.

One of the reasons the capital campaign model of involving as many volunteers as possible is so successful is that when people are engaged in the project, they are far more likely to contribute at a substantial level. As with all other volunteers, committee members must have the ability needed to fulfill their particular tasks in the campaign. Leadership Gift Committee members, for example, must have the ability to make a leadership gift, connections to others in the leadership gift category, and the willingness to ask others to join them in their investment. By following this strategy of engaging the Board fully, recruiting top leadership first, and then recruiting the "right people in the right seats on the bus" for other committee positions, the organization can effectively use volunteers in its capital campaign.

Summary

Most organizations face a capital campaign at one time or another. A capital campaign is always volunteer intensive. Some key volunteer roles in the campaign are as follows:

- Steering Committee.

- Campaign Chair.

- Campaign Cabinet.

- Committee Members.

Recruiting a top-notch Steering Committee and Campaign Cabinet is one of the keys to a successful campaign. The Campaign Cabinet will lead the effort to plan and implement the capital campaign.

It is crucial to have a campaign plan that contains an organizational chart with all of the various divisions that will be needed, along with position descriptions for each volunteer role. First, decide what seats need to be filled, and then recruit the right volunteers for each of these seats.

Qualities to look for in Cabinet Members include the following:

- Leadership qualities, including the ability to recruit and inspire others.

- Commitment to the mission, vision, and values of the organization.

- Ability to give of their time according to the campaign timeline for their particular committee.

- Respect of and connections in the community.

Further Reading

Dove, Kent. *Conducting a Successful Capital Campaign*. San Francisco: Jossey-Bass, 1988.

Lysakowski, Linda, and Judith Snyder. *Getting Ready for a Capital Campaign*. Alexandria, VA: Association of Fundraising Professionals, 2002.

Rosso, Henry. *Achieving Excellence in Fundraising*. San Francisco: Jossey-Bass, 1991.

EXHIBIT 3.1

Campaign Cabinet Organizational Chart

XYX Organization

"TITLE" CAPITAL CAMPAIGN

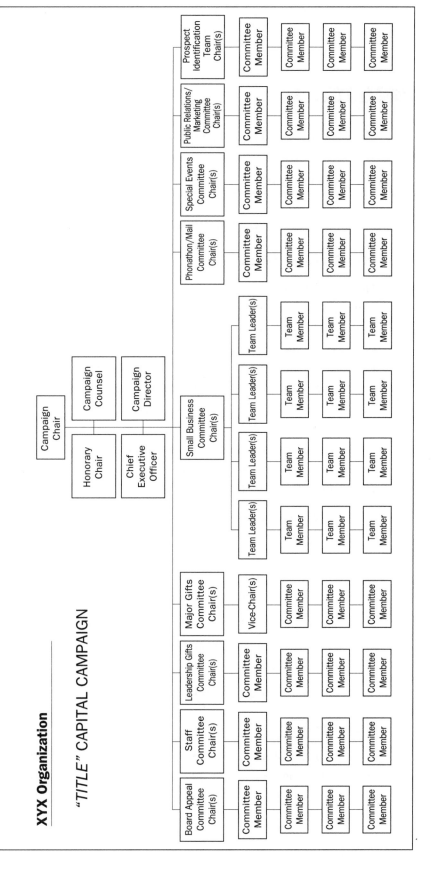

EXHIBIT 3.2

Capital Campaign Position Descriptions

XYZ ORGANIZATION

CAMPAIGN TITLE:

Chief Executive Officer

The role of the Chief Executive Officer in the campaign is absolutely critical. The Chief Executive Officer must devote approximately 50 percent of his or her time to this campaign effort throughout the duration of the campaign, make him- or herself available for key Lead and Major Gift calls (in this campaign a Lead Gift is defined as a gift over $100,000 and a Major Gift is defined as a gift between $25,000 and $100,000), not be afraid of "making the ask," and provide the visionary leadership that will be needed to encourage, inspire, and motivate the Campaign Cabinet and all volunteers involved in the campaign. Responsibilities for the Chief Executive Officer include the following:

- Select and recruit the chair for the campaign.

- Provide direction for the campaign.

- Provide support to the chair and committee members.

- Identify and solicit Lead Gift prospects.

- Provide information about the projects being funded, as needed to Campaign Counsel, Campaign Cabinet, and other campaign volunteers.

- Attend meetings of the Capital Campaign Cabinet.

Campaign Chair

The Campaign Chair is the acknowledged and recognized leader of the Capital Campaign, who personally subscribes to and supports the financial goals of the campaign, as well as encourages and stimulates the capabilities and generosity of others. A Campaign Steering Committee will assist enlistment of committee leadership in the form of a Campaign Cabinet. All leadership will be accountable to the Campaign Chair for the performance of their responsibilities. Responsibilities for the Campaign Chair include the following:

- Be the official spokesperson for the campaign.

- Chair the Campaign Cabinet meetings.

- Give leadership to the committee kickoff meeting.

- Provide leadership and assistance, as needed in soliciting lead, major, business, foundation, and individual gifts.

- Work with Campaign Counsel to bring the campaign to a successful conclusion on schedule.

The Campaign Chair is the representative of the organization's campaign and reflects its values, ideals, and objectives. The Chair brings status, inspiration, and motivation to the campaign.

Honorary Campaign Chair

The Honorary Campaign Chair (or Chairs) is the acknowledged and recognized honorary leader of the Capital Campaign, who personally subscribes to and supports the financial goals of the campaign, as well as encourages and stimulates the capabilities and generosity of others. Responsibilities of the Honorary Campaign Chair include the following:

- Be the honorary official spokesperson(s) for the campaign.

- Have set the example of leadership through outstanding leadership for the XYZ Organization community or through exemplary giving in support of the campaign.

The Honorary Campaign Chair is the representative of the organization's campaign and reflects its values, ideals, and objectives. The Honorary Chair brings status, inspiration, and motivation to the campaign.

continued on the next page

Campaign Cabinet Member

The Campaign Cabinet is responsible for guiding all aspects of the campaign. The Campaign Cabinet should consist of well-known and respected leaders in the community served by XYZ Organization. An outline of key leadership positions as well as a general position description for all Campaign Cabinet members follows.

Members of the Capital Campaign Cabinet will provide leadership and direction for the campaign. Members will be recruited from XYZ Organization constituents and will have the following responsibilities:

- Serve as chair, co-chair, or member of one of the Campaign Cabinet subcommittees.
- Recruit members to serve on various committees, as applicable.
- Make a meaningful gift to the campaign.
- Identify and solicit possible major donors to the campaign.
- Attend campaign events and functions.
- Attend monthly meetings of the Cabinet.
- Promote the campaign to the XYZ community.

Additionally, members will have the responsibilities outlined in the position description of the position filled on the Campaign Cabinet.

Board Gifts Committee Co-Chair

The Board Gifts Committee will play an integral role in ensuring that all members of the XYZ Organization family, including Board members of XYZ Organization, are involved by making full and early commitments to the campaign, setting an example to motivate others to follow. Responsibilities of the Board Gifts Committee Co-Chair include the following:

- Identify and recruit Board Gifts Committee of three to seven members.
- Establish goal for Board division.

- Make a presentation about the campaign to the full Board at a Board meeting.
- Sign a letter to be sent to all Board members in advance of the solicitation.
- Follow up with Board members regarding their commitments.
- Attend and report at monthly Campaign Cabinet meetings.

The Chair(s) of this committee will be a part of the Campaign Cabinet and will work closely with the Campaign Chair.

Staff Gifts Committee Chair

The Staff Gifts Committee will play an integral role in ensuring that all members of the XYZ Organization family, including staff members of XYZ Organization, are involved by making full and early commitments to the campaign as an example to motivate others to give. Responsibilities of the Staff Gifts Committee Chair include the following:

- Identify and recruit staff gifts team of approximately two to four staff members.
- Assist with evaluation of staff gift prospects.
- Assist with establishing goals for each staff division.
- Coordinate presentations at staff meetings about the campaign.
- Solicit approximately five to seven staff gift prospects.
- Attend and report at monthly Campaign Cabinet meetings.

The Chair(s) of this committee will be a part of the Campaign Cabinet and will work closely with the Campaign Chair.

Prospect Development and Evaluation Committee

The Prospect Development and Evaluation Committee will identify, select, and evaluate potential prospects in targeted markets for the Capital Campaign. The evaluation process will begin with those who have a previous giving history to XYZ Organization.

continued on the next page

Part of the intent of the campaign is to expand the giving base by adding new names of potential friends and donors. The Committee can be assured that all names submitted for evaluation and all work of the Prospect Development and Evaluation Committee will be treated in confidence. The Committee structure will entail several subcommittees representing specific market segments, including the following:

- Individuals.

- Businesses.

- Organizations.

Responsibilities of the Committee include the following:

- Develop a list of potential donors who will be evaluated regarding their ability to support this Capital Campaign.

- Concentrate the work of the Prospect Development and Evaluation Committee in the gift range of $10,000 and above.

- Establish a series of three to four meetings, at which time the potential prospects will be evaluated and qualified regarding their giving range and assigned to one of the soliciting committees by the category of Lead, Major, and Special Gifts.

- Evaluate the Committee's work throughout the campaign to determine if additional meetings will be needed.

The Chair(s) of this committee will be a part of the Campaign Cabinet working closely with the Campaign Chair.

Lead Gifts Committee

The Lead Gifts Committee will be responsible for soliciting the top prospects in the Capital Campaign. Lead Gift donors are those who are recognized to have the ability to commit $100,000 or more and will be solicited through this Committee. All solicitations shall be done on an individual, face-to-face basis and in an atmosphere that is conducive to thoughtful and serious consideration. This Committee will consist of the Chair(s) and an appropriate number of members to carry out the solicitation process of the prospects assigned to this committee. Responsibilities of the Lead Gifts Committee members include the following:

- Develop a strategy and prepare committee plans for a successful effort.
- Review the prospect list for completeness and accuracy.
- Review the suggested giving ranges as evaluated by the Prospect Development Committee.
- Establish a goal for this committee.
- Establish a timetable for conducting solicitations.
- Receive orientation and training in gift solicitation techniques.
- Establish a process for reporting and measuring progress toward the goal.

The Chair(s) will be a part of the Campaign Cabinet and will work closely with the Campaign Chair.

Major Gifts Committee

The Major Gifts Committee will be responsible for soliciting the major prospects in the Capital Campaign. Major Gift donors are those who are recognized to have the ability to commit $25,000 to $99,999 and will be solicited through this Committee. All solicitations shall be done on an individual, face-to-face basis and in an atmosphere that is conducive to thoughtful and serious consideration. This committee will consist of the Chair(s) and an appropriate number of members to carry out the solicitation process of the prospects assigned to this committee. Responsibilities of the Major Gifts Committee members include the following:

- Develop a strategy and prepare committee plans for a successful effort.
- Review the prospect list for completeness and accuracy.

continued on the next page

- Review the suggested giving ranges as evaluated by the Prospect Development Committee.

- Establish a goal for this committee.

- Establish a timetable for conducting solicitations.

- Receive orientation and training in gift solicitation techniques.

- Establish a process for reporting and measuring progress toward the goal.

The Chair(s) will be a part of the Campaign Cabinet and will work closely with the Campaign Chair.

Special Gifts Committee

The Special Gifts Committee will be responsible for soliciting prospects identified in the Special Gifts category in the Capital Campaign. Special Gift donors are those who are recognized to have the ability to commit $10,000 to $24,999 and will be solicited through this Committee. All solicitations shall be done on an individual, face-to-face basis and in an atmosphere that is conducive to thoughtful and serious consideration. (Suggested that one solicitor ask five others for gifts.) This committee will consist of the Chair(s) and an appropriate number of members to carry out the solicitation process of the prospects assigned to this committee. Responsibilities of the Special Gifts Committee members include the following:

- Develop a strategy and prepare committee plans for a successful effort.

- Review the prospect list for completeness and accuracy.

- Review the suggested giving ranges as evaluated by the Prospect Development Committee.

- Establish a goal for this committee.

- Establish a timetable for conducting solicitations.

- Receive orientation and training in gift solicitation techniques.

- Establish a process for reporting and measuring progress toward the goal.

The Chair will be a part of the Campaign Cabinet and will work closely with the Campaign Chair.

Vendor and Business Gifts Committee

The Vendor and Business Gifts Committee will be responsible for developing a solicitation strategy for each of the vendors identified as prospects in the Capital Campaign. This Committee will consist of the Chair(s), three Vice Chairs, and an appropriate number of members to carry out the process of soliciting the prospects selected by this Committee. Responsibilities of the Vendor and Business Gifts Committee members include the following:

- Develop a strategy and prepare committee plans for a successful effort.
- Review the vendors' list for completeness and accuracy.
- Create suggested request ranges and cross-reference them with the Prospect Development and Evaluation Committee before soliciting.
- Conduct additional prospect review and evaluation as appropriate.
- Establish a goal for this committee.
- Establish a timetable for submitting requests and visitation where appropriate.
- Assist in identifying individuals who can influence a decision and see if they can be visited to enlist their support and help in asking for the gift or in opening the door so others may ask for the gift.
- Receive solicitation training for asking for gifts.
- Where appropriate, be willing to meet with owners and representatives in presenting campaign objectives and requests.

continued on the next page

- Establish a process for reporting and measuring progress toward the goal.

The Chair(s) will be a part of the Campaign Cabinet and will work closely with the Campaign Chair.

Foundation Gifts Committee

The Campaign Director and Campaign Counsel will be responsible for developing a solicitation strategy for each of the foundation prospects in the Capital Campaign. This Committee will work closely with the Campaign Director and Campaign Counsel, who will carry out the process of foundation development with the prospects assigned to this committee. Responsibilities of the Foundation Gifts Committee members include the following:

- Develop a strategy and prepare committee plans for a successful effort.

- Review and identify the prospect list for foundations for completeness and accuracy.

- Review the suggested request ranges as provided through foundation research.

- Conduct additional foundation prospect review and evaluation as appropriate.

- Establish a goal for this committee.

- Establish a timetable for submitting written requests and visitation where appropriate.

- Review lists of prospective foundation funders with members of the Cabinet and Board to identify individuals who have links to trustees of the foundations or others who can influence a decision.

- Where appropriate, be willing to meet with foundation representatives in presenting campaign objectives and requests.

- Establish a process for reporting and measuring progress toward the goal.

The Chair(s) will be a part of the Campaign Cabinet and will work closely with the Campaign Chair.

Organizations Gifts Committee

The Organization Gifts Committee will be responsible for setting up solicitation of gifts with groups related to XYZ Organization or that may have an interest in the Capital Campaign. This will include affiliate groups such as auxiliary organizations of XYZ and professional and service clubs. Solicitations should be done, when possible, on an individual, face-to-face basis and in an atmosphere that is conducive to thoughtful and serious consideration. This committee will consist of the Chair(s) and an appropriate number of members to carry out the solicitation process of the prospects assigned to this committee. Responsibilities of the Organization Gifts Committee members include the following:

- Develop a strategy and prepare committee plans for a successful effort.

- Review the prospect lists for completeness and accuracy.

- Conduct additional prospect review and evaluation as appropriate.

- Establish a goal for this committee.

- Establish a timetable for conducting presentations/ solicitations.

- Receive orientation and training in gift solicitation techniques.

- Establish a process for reporting and measuring progress toward the goal.

The Chair(s) will be a part of the Campaign Cabinet and will work closely with the Campaign Chair.

continued on the next page

Special Events Committee

The Special Events Committee will develop and implement specific campaign promotional events and host cultivation activities in support of the Capital Campaign. Responsibilities of the Special Events Committee members include the following:

- Identify, plan, and develop special events to promote and support the Capital Campaign effort based on the campaign plan.
- Develop and plan hosted cultivation events to be implemented during the Campaign and in advance of the solicitation phase.
- Identify, recruit, orient, and coordinate with the hosts and hostesses for these cultivation events.
- Develop a kick-off event involving the appropriate campaign leadership.
- Develop an event calendar and coordinate with the campaign office.
- Coordinate event follow-up communications with the campaign office and the host/hostess of each social event.
- Develop, plan, and implement a victory celebration in cooperation with the XYZ Organization campaign office and the leadership of the Campaign Cabinet, upon campaign completion.

The Chair(s) will be a part of the Campaign Cabinet and will work closely with the Campaign Chair.

Public Relations Committee

The Public Relations Committee is responsible for the development and implementation of a Communication and Public Relations program to gain the attention and interest of potential donors, motivating them to support the Capital Campaign at the appropriate time. Responsibilities of the Public Relations Committee members include the following:

- Implement the Capital Campaign PR plan of action.
- Develop written materials, as needed, to support the public information program that may be specifically appropriate to the campaign effort.

- Create and produce a campaign video.
- Work with the staff and leaders of the campaign to create PowerPoint and/or DVD/CD for use at campaign meetings and presentations.
- Develop media and marketing strategies, as appropriate, to target markets and work with both print and electronic media to create publicity.
- Periodically evaluate their work and accomplishments to determine what additional activity needs to be undertaken to further position the campaign for success.

The Chair(s) will be a part of the Campaign Cabinet and will work closely with the Campaign Chair.

Business Appeal Team Chair

The Business Committee raises money from local businesses and corporations for the XYZ Organization Capital Campaign. Funds for this appeal may include gifts in kind, if they are appropriate for the project and meet the guidelines established in the Gift Acceptance Policies of XYZ Organization. The Business Appeal Committee will be involved in this fundraising effort between the months xxx and xxx. Team leaders will have the following responsibilities:

- Identify and help recruit approximately 10 team leaders.
- Assist with identification and evaluation of small to medium sized business prospects.
- Solicit team leaders for their gifts.
- Sign letter to mailed to all prospects.
- Attend and preside at business appeal kickoff meeting and report meetings.
- Attend and preside at victory celebration.

Business Team Leader

The Business Appeal Committee raises money from local businesses and corporations for the XYZ Organization Capital Campaign. Funds for

continued on the next page

this appeal may include gifts in kind, if they are appropriate for the project and meet the guidelines established in the Gift Acceptance Policies of XYZ Organization. The Business Appeal Committee will be involved in this fundraising effort between the months of xxx and xxx. Team leaders will have the following responsibilities:

- Identify and recruit approximately five team workers.
- Assist with identification and evaluation of business and corporate gift prospects by attending two prospect identification and rating sessions.
- Solicit their team members for their gifts to the annual fund.
- Advise and encourage team members.
- Solicit approximately three to five businesses.
- Attend and report at three to four report meetings and a final victory celebration.

Business Team Member

The Business Appeal Committee raises money from local business and corporations for the XYZ Organization Capital Campaign. Funds for this appeal may include gifts in kind, if they are appropriate for the project and meet the guidelines established in the Gift Acceptance Policies of XYZ Organizzation. The Business Appeal Committee will be involved in this fundraising effort between the months of xxx and xxx. Team leaders will have following responsibilities:

- Assist with identification and evaluation of business prospects.
- Attend kickoff meeting.
- Make a personal or corporate gift to the appeal.
- Solicit approximately five businesses.
- Report results to team leader in advance of the three to four report meetings.
- Attend a victory celebration.

CHAPTER 4

Volunteers in Other Fundraising Roles

After reading this chapter, you will be able to:

- List the various roles volunteers can fill in your organization's fundraising effort.
- Outline the number and types of volunteers needed in your organization's fundraising program.
- Develop a plan to use the capital campaign model for using volunteers in the annual appeal.

Volunteers in the Annual Fund

Most organizations understand and accept the concept of using volunteers in capital campaigns, but these same organizations often view the annual fund as strictly a staff-driven program. As outlined in Chapter 1, there are many ways volunteers can help drive the annual fund to new heights. All of the principles used in capital campaigns can be easily translated into a successful annual fund program.

One failure that is common in nonprofit organizations is that they do not develop a compelling case for support for their annual fund. This task is critical to developing strong volunteer involvement. If volunteers are unaware of or uncommitted to the case, they will be unable to raise money to support this case. There must be a compelling case for support, adequate support materials developed from that case, and involvement of volunteers in the case development. Volunteers who are involved in the development of the case are more likely to support it and present it to potential donors with enthusiasm. Volunteers become involved in the development of the case for support through surveys, focus groups, and one-on-one interviews.

Donor and volunteer surveys can help determine what areas of the program interest donors. Surveys can be done through the mail, in person, by telephone, or via the Internet. Some organizations have hired marketing firms to survey people at malls or door-to-door when a random sampling is desired. For an organization that wants to focus on what its donors or volunteers think about the case, direct mail or telephone are more effective approaches because the target audience can be identified and reached. Advanced technologies have made surveying fairly simple in today's world. Using Survey Monkey or similar programs, Internet surveys are fairly easy to develop, implement, and analyze because the results are automatically tabulated by the service providing the survey.

In-person interviews on a one-on-one basis are always the most effective method of surveying, just as in asking for the gift, but this method requires more staff or volunteer time. In a capital campaign, the preliminary case for support is almost always tested through the planning study (or feasibility study), but this method can also be used in an annual campaign case statement. For many organizations embarking on their first major fundraising effort, a planning study may be the best way to test their case.

A focus group is another way to test the strength of the case for support. This method brings together a group of volunteers, especially those who will be

The Planning Study

One organization, a quasi-governmental agency, actually conducted a planning study to determine if setting up a development office and embarking on private fundraising would be accepted by its community. Because this organization was a publicly funded organization, it was concerned that private foundations, individuals, and corporations would feel that their tax dollars already supported this entity and would not be likely to provide funding for any of its initiatives. However, during the study it became apparent that the organization did have a compelling case for support and that almost all of the interviewees said they would support the establishment of a development office and the launching of private fundraising efforts to fund the initiatives outlined in the case.

involved in using the case to raise money. A facilitator presents the case and then invites input from the volunteers. Focus groups must be carefully orchestrated. A facilitator, either staff consultant or volunteer (if there is a volunteer available who is skilled in conducting focus groups), must coordinate the session. It is important to keep questions open-ended and facilitate dialogue, ensuring participation from all attendees. If the right volunteer is found for the facilitation task, this becomes a great way to involve volunteers on both sides of the table—participants and facilitator. Often someone from the marketing department of a corporation can be enlisted to volunteer as a facilitator.

Simone Joyeaux says, "Engaging volunteers in appropriate and meaningful ways must be the biggest challenge faced by nonprofit organizations." For many organizations, the annual fund involves direct mail, possibly a telephone campaign, and sometimes a corporate appeal. Many organizations, however, think of these as staff-driven activities, and they may only use volunteers to stuff mailings or

Focus Groups

One organization developed its case for support, translated it into a PowerPoint presentation, and then invited a group of about 20 volunteers to a focus group. The focus group participants were treated to a luncheon at the agency, greeted by the Executive Director and the Volunteer Chair of Publicity, and then shown the PowerPoint presentation. After the showing, a few open-ended questions were asked: "What do you think of the case as it was presented? Are there areas of our program that should be emphasized more or less? Would this case prompt a donation from you?" Volunteer input led to several changes in the case, and the organization saved itself money and potential embarrassment by not jumping into developing elaborate fundraising materials until they were assured the case was a strong one.

work the phones. Nonprofits that are successful in meeting the challenge to give volunteers a meaningful and rewarding part in their development programs involve volunteers in every aspect of their fundraising efforts, starting with the annual fund.

Having a chair(s) of the annual fund each year, with the same leadership drive and energy as described in the capital campaign model in Chapter 2, can lend a special credibility to the organization when approaching donors. Having donors recognize that the organization has successfully recruited volunteers who have made a commitment to the organization's fundraising is a commodity that you could not purchase with the best and highest-paid staff person available. The chairs of the annual fund will guide the overall appeal, which might include a corporate appeal, a major gift effort, a phone-a-thon, a direct mail campaign, and possibly even special events. As in capital campaigning, the overall chair(s) will be responsible for helping to recruit various committee chairs (e.g., corporate, phone-a-thon), inspiring other volunteers to greatness, making a significant contribution, signing letters, and presiding over meetings and events relating to the annual fund.

In today's world, everyone seems be involved 24/7 with work and family activities. Just finding individuals who have the passion for the nonprofit organization *and* a few hours a month to volunteer can often be the most difficult part of the equation. As a rule, one or two volunteers will quickly demonstrate leadership skills that set them apart from the group. If staff members take the time to work closely with these leaders, they will prove to be the greatest motivators of the development team.

Using Volunteers in the Board Appeal

The first effort in any annual fund effort should be the Board appeal. This segment of the annual appeal is discussed in the next chapter.

Using Volunteers in the Direct Mail Component of the Annual Fund

Direct mail can certainly utilize volunteers to stuff mailings, and in fact numerous groups (e.g., senior groups, youth groups) are happy for an activity to help them meet their service requirements or fill time. But volunteers can also be used in other, more meaningful ways during a direct mail effort. Receiving a letter written by the parent of a child killed by a drunk driver, a student on a scholarship, a recovering addict, etc., is far more motivating to donors than receiving a letter from the CEO or other staff member of the organization. Consider using volunteers to draft a letter that can be edited by the staff. Or, the staff can draft a letter with the key elements and then ask the volunteers to add their own personal touch.

Annual Fund Volunteers

One development professional cites a volunteer success story that happened while serving as the director of development at a very young college-prep school:

"Before my arrival, the school had always solicited parents for contributions to the annual fund via a letter from a Board member followed by a phone-a-thon, and they had usually met their goal!

When I arrived, I was tasked with tweaking the annual fund and striving to surpass the current goal. My approach involved turning the annual fund mail appeal into an annual fund campaign with a campaign case, theme, leadership gift, timeline, goal, giving levels, brochure, letterhead, and volunteer leaders for each grade. Additionally, I recruited several grandparents because they had the passion and the time to volunteer! Because the school was young, we had only a few alumni, but we began the process of getting them involved in the campaign. Our key elements of participation included making our own gifts first, personalized letters from each volunteer to the parents or alumni of the grade they represented, and training for the phone-a-thon. We even had competition between the grade levels and the faculty and staff. (Of course, I solicited the staff, which had never happened before.) Our annual fund campaign was very successful, and we did surpass our goal!

Most importantly, the night of the phone-a-thon several of the volunteers expressed an interest in serving on next year's campaign, and they were already talking about others they could get involved. The annual fund is something that has to be done every year. Developing a written case and plan that will energize the volunteers and the staff will help to raise the entire process to a new level and keep everyone involved."

Volunteers should also review the list of direct mail constituents and select letters for people they know personally, to which they can add a personal note asking for support. Be aware, however, that adding personal notes to letters disqualifies those mailings from bulk mail rates from the U.S. Postal Service. However, personalizing a letter instead of using a cold direct mail approach will result in a much greater return on investment, so it may be well worth the approximately 20 cents difference in postal rates. Another way to effectively use volunteers in a meaningful way is to hold a focus group with constituents and have them provide input into the direct mail package as it is being developed. Ask volunteers how they would respond to the carrier (outside) envelope, the letter, and any enclosures that are planned to be included in the package.

IN THE REAL WORLD

Volunteers in a Direct Mail Program

One organization, seeking to increase its annual giving, engaged a consultant to analyze what it could do to improve results. Several new initiatives were started: a major gift appeal, a phone-a-thon, and a new approach to the direct mail program. The organization had previously sent a "dear friend of (the cause)" letter, and the executive director had always signed this letter. The new approach involved enlisting a high-profile national figure to serve as honorary chair of the mail appeal. Draft letters were faxed and e-mailed to this person's office in another state for his approval. A photo and signature were received from the honorary chair, and these were used to make the appeal more personal. In fact, because this was a nationally known figure, his photo was used on the outside (carrier) envelope, with a one-line teaser to entice people to open the envelope. This volunteer agreed to have his scanned signature used to sign the letters after his approval. Using a volunteer signer, especially one who was nationally recognized, helped this organization increase its mail response by 20 percent and raise 35 percent more dollars than it had in the previous year.

Using Volunteers for Telephone Fundraising in the Annual Fund

For organizations with thousands of potential donors to be called, it is generally recommonded that they engage a professional telephone fundraising firm. (For a list of firms that meet AFP standards and do not work on a percentage basis, see the AFP Consultant Directory at *www.afpnet.org*). However, volunteers are often more effective when the organization has a smaller number of people to be called. It is critical to remember, though, that volunteers in a phone-a-thon must be carefully trained and provided with scripts and other materials they will need to be successful on the phone. In some states (e.g., Pennsylvania), telephone fundraisers are required to state whether they are professional solicitors. People identifying themselves as volunteers in the opening statement to the person being called often have the advantage of being accepted as people who have given of their time because they believe in the cause.

Volunteers can also be invited to participate in thank-a-thons. This activity is particularly effective for getting Board members involved in the fundraising activities of the organization. Board members who have never done fundraising can begin to develop a comfort level with fundraising by learning how to develop a relationship with donors by calling major donors. Other volunteers can also be involved in this activity, which binds the volunteers and the donors even closer to the organization because the volunteers are directly involved in telling donors how their money is being used. When feasible, this is effectively done by recipients of the organization's services.

Using Volunteers for a Business Appeal in the Annual Fund

Some organizations attempt to solicit corporations and businesses by using direct mail or sending a cold grant proposal. Corporation and business appeals are far more effective when executives are contacted by peer volunteers. An annual corporate appeal, done through face-to-face, personal solicitations, is an area that many nonprofits have tried and found to be the most successful way to approach businesses and corporations. Volunteers will enable organizations to reach many business leaders who have previously been impossible to meet, because the volunteers are calling on someone they know and with whom they have a personal and/or business relationship.

In a corporate appeal, there can be two or more co-chairs, each of whom is expected to recruit team leaders, who in turn will recruit five team members for their team. In this way fundraising can be spread out to the largest number of volunteers, assigning no more than five prospects to any one volunteer. So, if the organization has 200 small businesses it wants to approach during its annual fund drive, the formula would be that the organization needs 40 volunteers to approach these businesses. A plan might go something like this:

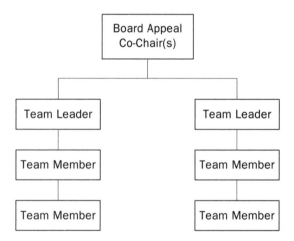

Almost every organization has one or two overenthusiastic volunteers who tend to bite off more than they can chew. These volunteers know everyone in town generally and sometimes just want to impress the rest of the volunteers with the number of contacts they have. Other times they are just classic overachievers who think they can tackle a list of 20 prospects and solicit them effectively. When this happens, the best approach is to ask these volunteers to select the five best prospects, because it is important to maximize their time and get the best

Small Business Appeal Plan

- Number of prospects to be contacted—400.

- Number of volunteers needed—80 (400 divided by 5).

- Number of team leaders needed—16 (80 divided by 5).

- Number of team leaders to be recruited by each Co-Chair—8 (16 divided by 2).

- Number of Co-Chairs to be recruited by Staff or Volunteer Annual Fund Chair—2.

results for their team. Once these people have successfully completed these five calls, then ask them to come back and start on their next list of five.

Using Volunteers for Special Events

In almost every organization, special events rely heavily on volunteer committees. Most special events are both staff and volunteer intensive. Volunteers usually serve

Kay Sprinkel Grace recommends that volunteer teams should have three goals to reach in their fundraising efforts:

- 100% contact with all prospects assigned.

- 100% of calls completed within the established timelines.

- Minimum dollar amount raised by each team.

IN THE REAL WORLD

Volunteers in the Corporate Appeal

One organization held an effective business community appeal each year, using approximately 150 volunteers who were recruited by means of the Chair and Vice Chair recruiting 20 to 25 team captains, who in turn recruited teams of three to seven people. Following the principle of not having any one team member contact more than five to seven prospects, these teams met early in the fiscal year to identify potential donors from a list of businesses the organization had developed. Volunteers were asked to select businesses with which they have a personal relationship and to contact only those businesses with which they knew they could get an appointment. Prospect lists were reviewed and updated annually as new volunteers became involved. Using this method, the organization began with a small corps of volunteers raising $4,000 in the first year and grew the program to a successful campaign raising more than $300,000 within about six years.

in a variety of capacities on special event committees. As with any type of fundraising effort, leadership is critical to success. Finding the right chair for the special event committee is the first step toward a successful event. The chair must be someone who is well organized, can follow timelines and meet deadlines, and who inspires other committee members to be diligent and tireless in their efforts. A special event committee chair can make or break the event. Committee members likewise need to be carefully selected for their abilities in different areas (e.g., organizational skills; handling seating arrangements; working with restaurants, caterers, musicians, etc.; special skills relating to the type of event— golf tournaments, art auctions, marathon running events), all will benefit from having a person with talents and interests in that area. Chapter 3 discusses developing position descriptions and the recruitment of volunteers.

Using Volunteers in the Grants Process

Staff or outside consultants usually prepare grant proposals, except in small organizations where there may not be staff available and volunteers step in to fill this role. However, proposals to foundations and corporations still need that personal touch. One way to give volunteers on the board or development committee a meaningful part in grant fundraising is to review the list of potential funders with a committee and/or the board as a whole to determine where there may be personal contacts. A list should be developed showing the trustees of the foundations or corporate contact for potential funders. Asking volunteers to review this list and identify any trustees with whom they have a personal contact or companies with which they may do business will help put a more personalized appeal together for that foundation. Furthermore, volunteers should be invited to attend meetings with potential funders, to help add credibility to the organization, and speak to the funders from the point of view of volunteers who have committed their time and money to the organization.

Using Volunteers to Make Major Gift Asks

Although volunteers can play numerous roles in the annual fundraising program, perhaps none is more critical than the role of volunteers in identifying, cultivating, and soliciting major donors. Professional fundraisers are trained in all aspects of fundraising and have a major role to play in the ask, but volunteers bring a special perspective to this role that should not be overlooked. In most cases, prospective donors will relate to an ask from a volunteer in a totally different way. For many donors, the asker is one of the most important factors in determining the commitment they will make. Most people like to be asked by someone they know, a colleague or friend; sometimes even a relative has much more clout than professional fundraisers may have with individuals. Especially in the corporate world, prospective donors want to be invited by their peers to join them in investing in a good organization and its programs.

The definition of a major donor is different for every organization; it may be $100, $100,000, or anywhere in between. But once the amount of a major gift is determined, volunteers can be effective in implementing a major gift program for any organization, regardless of the organization's size, the size of a major gift, or the number of constituents.

Before volunteers can be expected to do major gift fundraising, however, a process of strategy, education, and training must take place. First, begin with holding strategy sessions in which the key elements of the ask are outlined. For an organization that does not already have any constituents it considers major donors, this work begins by involving volunteers in the identification process. A Brainstorming Form (see Exhibit 4.1 at the end of this chapter) can help with this task. Ask Board members and/or other volunteers, those on the Development Committee or Annual Fund Committee, to help identify people who could be major donors for the organization. After a process of identification and cultivation has taken place and prospects are ready for the ask, volunteers should be brought together again for a Screening and Rating Session, in which prospects are assigned to the best person to make the ask, and ask amounts are identified for each prospect. Exhibit 4.2, a sample form for this purpose, can also be found at the end of this chapter. Volunteers for major gifts fundraising will need training in scheduling the appointment and making the ask. As has often been said, major gift fundraising relies on having "the right person, asking the right person, at the right time, in the right way, for the right amount, and for the right purpose."

The role of the volunteer in this process is to help develop the best strategy to approach a donor. Why is the volunteer role essential? Consider the three key elements:

1. *Ability.* Although a professional fundraiser can do all the research in the world, some things may only be known to a select few people and are not public knowledge. One should never expect a volunteer to violate confidentiality, but volunteers are often the best source of information about prospective donors: Is their business doing well? Do they have family issues

TIPS & TECHNIQUES

The three essential elements of a major gift are the following:

- ***Ability.*** How much *could* the prospect give?

- ***Linkage.*** Who has the best connection to this prospect?

- ***Interest.*** What are the prospect's special areas of interest that might be effectively used to generate interest in this organization, program, or project?

that may require funds to be conserved right now? Are they anticipating a huge inheritance? During the screening process, volunteers can often help determine the ability of prospects to give, which, along with their propensity to give, will be critical factors in determining the size of the ask.

2. *Linkage.* "It's not what you know, but who you know!" During the strategy session, finding the best possible linkage with the prospective donors is one of the key outcomes. Often an organization may have numerous links to a prospective donor, but during the strategy season, the organization must determine who is the best person to make the ask. Is it a close friend, the business colleague, or the brother-in-law? The person or team who has the best chance of successfully making a call must be determined.

3. *Interest.* Volunteers often have an intimate knowledge of the interests of the prospective donors. One volunteer may know them well on a personal level and know that they have a real love for animals and that any appeal for a cause relating to saving endangered species or rescuing a breed of dog would be the key to unlocking that major gift. Another volunteer may have solicited prospects for another organization and knows that they traditionally give to the arts, so if the appeal were for an arts group, the

prospects would be likely to give more. Yet other volunteers may be relatives of prospective donors, who know that they have a soft spot for special needs children, because there is a family member with a special needs child, so an ask for this type of program would be likely to generate a good response from the prospect.

All of this is accomplished in the strategy or screening process. Kent Dove says, "Prospect rating must be done by volunteers in order to validate the work done by staff." To involve volunteers in this process, there are a few simple rules.

 TIPS & TECHNIQUES

Volunteers for screening sessions should include:

- Those who are likely to have knowledge of the prospective donor list.
- People who have worked on fundraising efforts for other organizations.
- Bankers and/or CPAs, who are often good sources of information on businesses and individuals.

The session itself should use the following guidelines:

- Volunteers included in this session may or may not be the same volunteers the organization will be using to contact these prospective donors.
- Confidentiality must be stressed.
- Names should be reviewed one-by-one, as a group.
- A facilitator (usually not a volunteer) should be used to control the discussion and keep it from becoming a gossip session.
- A limited number of prospects should be reviewed at each session (50 to 100 is generally a good number).

The screening and rating process can be carried out in other ways, also using volunteers. One way is for a staff person to develop a list of potential donors and meet with volunteers one-on-one to review the list and get input on an individual basis, which is often more comfortable for the volunteers. This can be done with dialogue between the staff and volunteers or done silently by the volunteers. However, this method loses the group dynamics that can be helpful when differing views exist about a prospect's ability, linkage, or interest. This method will also require more staff time because each volunteer is interviewed separately.

Another method is to do a silent screening, whereby the group is assembled and lists are reviewed privately without discussion, and then the lists are collated and evaluated by staff. Again, this process will take more staff time and is missing the interaction of the group. However, any or all of these methods may be employed until the organization finds the one that is best suited for its purposes and organizational personality.

IN THE REAL WORLD

Screening and Rating Sessions

One organization that was conducting a screening and rating session in preparation for a major gifts appeal found what it thought would be a major donor prospect—a highly regarded and successful surgeon in the community. However, another physician in the room, when it was time to discuss this prospect, simply said, "I don't believe we should approach this prospect right now. The timing is not good. There are some issues I cannot discuss, but trust me, we should not approach him right now." It turned out later that this prospect was in the process of a divorce and, once the dust had settled, the prospect was approached and did make a significant gift to the organization. However, this gift may have been lost if the prospect had been approached at the wrong time.

Using Volunteers in Planned Giving Efforts

Although planned giving is often thought of as a staff or consultant's role because of the specialized knowledge involved, volunteers can help with the planned giving efforts of an organization in numerous ways. A committee of volunteer professional advisors can be effective in teaching the staff about various planned giving instruments, developing effective promotional materials for planned giving, making connections for the organization with potential planned giving donors, and conducting planned giving seminars.

Volunteers who have already made a planned gift are the best spokespersons for the organization's planned giving program and should be invited to help identify other potential donors and to introduce these donors to the organization. Volunteers can be asked to give testimonials or write an article for the organization's newsletter about why they made a planned gift to the organization.

IN THE REAL WORLD

Volunteers in Planned Giving

One public television station has a Planned Giving Committee, made up of estate planning professionals, which has assisted the station in setting up its estate gift program. These professionals volunteer their time to present no-cost/no-obligation estate planning seminars in the community, sponsored by the station. They have recorded on-air announcements, met with potential donors, and helped the station set up its recognition program for estate donors, the Silver Legacy Society. This program has generated $36.5 million in gift expectancies in its six-year history! One gift matured in 2004 and was used to open the station's Endowment Fund. This program and this committee won a PBS Fundraising Award for Excellence in 2002 for its outstanding achievements. The station's development director says that were it not for this committee, the station would not have a planned giving program in place at all.

Summary

Most of the principles that apply to capital campaigns can easily be translated into the annual fund and other fundraising efforts, especially the role of volunteers. Some important things to remember when recruiting volunteers to help with the annual fund are the following:

- There must be a compelling case for the annual fund and appropriate fundraising materials to be used by volunteers.

- Volunteers must be given clear goals for their fundraising involvement.

- It is crucial to get the right people "on the bus and in the right seats."

Major gift fundraising requires the involvement of volunteers to identify, cultivate, and solicit major donor prospects. Volunteers should play a lead role in the screening and rating process to help identify the three key components of a major gift:

- Linkage.

- Ability.

- Interest.

Further Reading

Collins, James C., and Jerry I. Porras. *Built to Last.* New York: HarperCollins, 1994.

Collins, Jim. *Good to Great.* New York: HarperCollins, 2001.

Grace, Kay Sprinkel. *Beyond Fundraising.* New York: John Wiley & Sons, 1997.

Joyeaux, Simone. *Building Profitable Relationships That Last.* Gaithersburg, MD: Aspen, 1997.

EXHIBIT 4.1

Brainstorming Form

Potential Donors for Our Organization

Your Name: _____

Category	Name & Address	Potential Major Donor Y or N	I will contact this person Y or N
My accountant			
My car dealer			
My banker(s)			
My attorney			
Members of my professional association			
My insurance agent			
My doctor(s)			
My dentist(s)			
Members of a service club to which I belong			

continued on the next page

Category	Name & Address	Potential Major Donor Y or N	I will contact this person Y or N
Neighbors			
Relatives			
Clients/ customers of mine			
Politicians I know			

People with whom I worship			
People with whom I work			
People with whom I went to school			
Parents of children with whom my children go to school			

continued on the next page

Category	Name & Address	Potential Major Donor Y or N	I will contact this person Y or N
My realtor			
People with whom I do business			
People with whom I play sports			
People I know support other charities			

People who have asked me to support their favorite charity			
People I know who volunteer for other nonprofit organizations			
Others			

EXHIBIT 4.2

Screening Form

XYX Organization

"CAMPAIGN THEME"

Name, Address Phone Number	Relationship with XYZ	Area of Interest	Suggested Ask Amount	Suggested Solicitor	Notes

CHAPTER 5

The Role of the Board in Fundraising

 After reading this chapter, you will be able to:

- List the critical elements in involving the Board in fundraising.
- Develop a plan to recruit Board members who will actively participate in fundraising.
- Structure a Development Committee.
- Determine what other auxiliary boards may be needed and how to structure them, when appropriate.

The Board as Volunteer Fundraisers

The Board has a special role in the fundraising initiative for any organization. Other volunteers will not be enthusiastic about getting involved in fundraising unless they see leadership by example coming from the Board of Directors.

However, before the Board members can be successful at fundraising, or even at governing the organization, they must buy into the mission of the organization and be fully committed to it. The Board is responsible for developing, reviewing, refining, and adjusting (if necessary) the mission statement of the organization. Boards should periodically go through a full strategic planning process in which the mission, vision, and values are reviewed (or developed if they are not already in place) (Lysakowski, *Building an Effective Board of Directors*).

It is essential to bring in an outside facilitator to guide the organization through this process. Volunteers can effectively serve as the facilitator of a strategic planning process, especially if the organization does not have the funds to hire a consultant for this process. Volunteers for this task must be carefully selected. The facilitator needs to be skilled and experienced in leading groups and in the planning process. However, local businesses or universities will often lend their planning officers to help smaller nonprofits through the planning process.

IN THE REAL WORLD

Volunteers in the Strategic Planning Process

A small museum, which was just beginning a new phase in its organizational life span and preparing to do a major fundraising campaign, recognized that strategic planning was one of its first priorities. A Board member, who was president of a major local financial institution, loaned the museum his Senior Vice President for Planning to lead the museum Board through the planning process. Working with the Museum Director and Director of Development, the loaned executive conducted an all-day planning retreat at a nearby museum and helped the Board establish a vision, short- and long-term goals, and strategies to help achieve its goals.

Board Giving and Fundraising—Give, Get, or Get Off?

The Give, Get, or Get Off model has been traditional wisdom for Board giving, but a new model that organizations may want to consider is outlined in *Building an Effective Board of Directors:* the Gather, Get Ready, and Grow model.

Gather: Reaching Consensus about Fundraising

For many organizations, it may be difficult to think of their Board as a fundraising board, but it is important to remember that all Boards can be fundraising boards when properly recruited, trained, and motivated.

A basic starting point is getting Board consensus that fundraising is a priority. If the Board does not accept its fundraising role as a priority for the

TIPS & TECHNIQUES

Using the Gather, Get Ready, and Grow model, any Board can be a fundraising board:

- *Gather.* The first step is to get all of the Board in agreement that fundraising is a responsibility of the Board.

- *Get Ready.* The next step is to prepare the Board for fundraising.

- *Grow.* With training and preparation, the Board can then grow into a fundraising board that will be able to fulfill the organization's vision through a more effective development program.

organization, then it may be necessary to bring in an outside consultant or a Board member from another organization to educate the Board on its role in fundraising for the organization. Like the model of using a volunteer for the strategic planning process, the volunteer chosen to lead the Board into its fundraising role must be carefully selected. A Board member from a successful fundraising organization in the community can often inspire other Board members. As a volunteer who has been successful at motivating his or her own Board to fundraise, this volunteer can speak from personal experience about how it works.

Once the Board accepts its fundraising role, the next step is to have Board members *put their money where their heart is*. Board giving should always be a requirement for any organization. If the Board does not support the organization financially, it will be difficult to convince others to support it and impossible for the Board to ask others to give. Many funders will require 100 percent Board giving before considering a request for funding from an organization. The annual Board Appeal should be the first fundraising activity of the fiscal year. Before asking anyone else to support the organization, it is critical to show that 100 percent of the Board has made its commitment. The Board Appeal is conducted much the same as any other fundraising appeal. Start by recruiting a team of Board members; usually the Board chair and members of the development committee are the solicitation team. If one Board member can be identified as one who "gets it" about fundraising, this person should lead the Development Committee. Bring this group together to evaluate each Board member's past giving and giving potential. Assign an ask amount and a solicitor to each Board member. A realistic Board Appeal goal is developed from this initial screening session; however, the entire Board should have input so they support this goal. A letter from the Board chair should precede the ask, stressing the importance of 100 percent giving at the Board level. As with any major donor ask, Board asks should be done in person, ensuring that the importance of this appeal is understood by each Board member.

The Board Appeal

One organization, after going through a development audit, realized that the Board's role in fundraising was practically nonexistent and that the first step in its development plan would be to motivate, energize, and train the Board for its new fundraising role.

The first step was to do an annual Board Appeal. A team of three Board members met with the executive director, director of development, and consultant to evaluate the individual Board members' potential for giving and to determine a goal for the Board Appeal. When this group first came together, they were reluctant to estimate what they thought other Board members could give, but once they realized it was the only way they would make their goal, they settled down to the task. Almost immediately, it became apparent that one Board member could give a substantial amount compared to the rest of the Board members. This Board member was approached first to get his input on the Board goal, the plan for the Board Appeal, and to make the first gift to the Board Appeal. The Board member, recognizing that other Board members would not be able to give at his level yet wanting to use his gift to inspire them to give at a meaningful level, proposed that he give his gift as a challenge, contingent on the Board Appeal reaching its goal. This incentive spurred on Board members to make stretch gifts, and a Board that had never been asked to give or ask before rose to the occasion, exceeding its goal and building an enthusiasm for fundraising. This enthusiasm carried over into the first attempt for this organization to cultivate and solicit major donors, and they enlisted Board members to host cultivation events to introduce new prospective donors to the organization.

Get Ready: Getting the Board Involved in Identifying, Cultivating, and Soliciting Donors

Once the Board Appeal is complete, it is time to move on to preparing the Board members to go out and talk to others about supporting the organization. If the organization already has a pool of donors, this task will be a little easier. If not, the brainstorming exercise described in Chapter 4 can be a starting point for getting the Board involved. Many organizations ask their Board members to develop a list of 10 or 15 names of people they think would support the organization; however, few Board members ever complete this task. Giving them a blank slate is not the best way to go. Bringing the Board together and giving them the tools to spark ideas will be much more successful.

Board members can also be helpful in cultivating existing donors to move to the next level. Penelope Burk says, "Most board members only interact with donors who have already made gifts of significant value. While these donors definitely need and deserve acknowledgement from the top of the organization, reserving leadership volunteers' influence for these donors severely limits board members' ability to impact overall fundraising performance."

Involving Board members in cultivating existing donors is critical; the Board should regularly do a thank-a-thon to medium-sized donors. This can be done in a group setting just as the organization would plan a phone-a-thon to ask for dollars. Or Board members can be given a list of midrange donors to contact each month, thanking them for their gifts.

 IN THE REAL WORLD

The "Thank-a-Thon"

One organization, a health agency whose mission was to promote organ donation, had a Board member whose daughter had received an organ transplant. This Board member suggested to the organization that he call all donors of $10 or more during the past year to thank them for their gift and for the fact that he could now watch his daughter grow up. Imagine the increase in donations from the recipients of a call like that!

Grow: Help the Board Grow in its Fundraising Ability

The final step in preparing the Board members to do fundraising is to train them in fundraising theory and techniques. A Board member or staff member from an organization that is successful in fundraising can often lead and inspire the Board to get involved in this endeavor. Even if they have been involved in fundraising for other organizations, Board members need to be given materials and training specific to the organization to be successful. Having a compelling case for support, written materials such as brochures, fact sheets, and pledge cards, and adequate training can help take the fear out of fundraising for most Boards and other volunteers. This process will be further described in Chapter 6.

Recruiting a Fundraising Board

The Board's unique role in fundraising must be taken into account when recruiting Board members. In advising grassroots Boards, this author suggested,

IN THE REAL WORLD

Every Board Member Has a Sphere of Influence

One Board that thought it had no influence or affluence among its ranks was surprised when preparing for a capital campaign and looking for major donors for the project. During a screening session, the name of a successful and philanthropic attorney was on the list. It turned out that one of the Board members, a quiet, unassuming woman who was a factory worker, was his cousin and was able to secure a gift to the campaign from this attorney.

First, the board needs to understand development and what it does for the organization, as well as their role in the development process. Start by holding a briefing session at a board meeting—board orientation is a good time to introduce this to new board members. Explain how important development is to the organization and what unfunded programs need support from private donors. Explain the function of the development office and how the board and staff work together as a team to raise money. This is a good time to introduce board members to the fact that most giving comes from individuals. (The giving charts from Giving USA will be helpful handouts or PowerPoint presentations for U.S. organizations—*www.AAFRC.org.*)

Board training will be discussed in more detail later.

For most organizations, the Board's reluctance to fundraise is systemic; it starts in the recruitment process. If Boards were recruited with clear expectations of their fundraising role, many frustrations on the part of Board and staff would be eliminated. The first step is to include fundraising in the Board position description (a sample can be found in Exhibit 5.1 at the end of the chapter), but just writing it down is not enough. The Board recruiters must have an open and honest conversation with potential Board members about the expectations of the organization in all areas, but especially fundraising. A nominating committee that is reluctant to do fundraising, making it even more difficult to talk to others about their fundraising role, often worsens the issue of a reluctant Board. The leaders of the Board, the chair or president and the Development Committee chair, must all be committed to fundraising, as well as those who will be recruiting Board members. For this reason, it is suggested to nonprofits that they rethink their nominating process. In fact, in advice given to Charity Channel subscribers, this author says,

> One of the best pieces of advice for any nonprofit organization is to get rid of your Nominating Committee. For most organizations, the Nominating Committee has two primary functions: to fill vacant Board seats and to elect officers of the Board. In many cases, this committee is an ad hoc committee appointed by the President or Chair a few months before terms are due to

expire. Often by the time the Board Chair appoints a Nominating Committee, most of the Board members are busy with other committees and the
nominating task seems to fall to someone who has not been tremendously
involved in other Board work. As a result, those selected for the Nominating
Committee may not be the best and brightest of the Board members. The
attitude is sometimes, "Well, how much harm can they do on a Nominating
Committee?" The answer is "a lot!"

Instead of a Nominating Committee, the recommended approach is to have
a year-round Board Resource Committee. This committee can also be called
the Governance Committee or the Committee on Directorship. Whatever the
title, the important things to remember about this committee are as follows:

- It should meet year-round.

- It needs to be chaired by the strongest person on the Board (and one
  who understands and is committed to fundraising).

- Its duties include conducting an assessment of Board performance, both
  the Board as a whole and individual Board members.

- It is responsible for developing or refining Board position descriptions.

- It evaluates the needs of the Board and develops a profile of the kinds of
  people that are needed to fill vacancies on the Board.

- It works with the Board to help find the right people to fill Board
  positions.

- It ensures diversity on the Board.

- It implements, along with senior staff members of the organization,
  Board orientation.

- It is responsible for ongoing education of the Board.

The Board Resource Committee is perhaps the most important committee
of the Board, *not an afterthought*. Once in place, this committee should first

complete a grid analyzing current strengths and weaknesses of the Board. Board members should be listed, according to the years their terms expire, and diversity indicators listed (e.g., ethnicity, gender, geographic location). Skills, talents, and areas of special expertise should also be listed, along with giving ability and contacts with various groups such as media, funders, and government agencies. Once this grid is complete, the committee can then determine where there are gaps in Board diversity, skills, and abilities. A profile can then be developed for recruitment of new Board members.

Staff and other volunteers can be involved in the recruitment process for most volunteers. For Board members, the invitation to join the Board must come from other Board members, in particular the Nominating Committee, Governance Committee, Board Development Committee, or Board Resource Committee. These committee titles are used interchangeably, but the term Nominating Committee often indicates an ad hoc committee that meets only when it is time to recruit new Board members. For the process of Board recruitment to be effective, the nominating process should be part of an ongoing effort to identify, cultivate, and recruit Board members through a committee with a more permanent status and one whose name imparts this permanency. A position description for such a committee is in Exhibit 5.2 at the end of this chapter.

Board members cannot be expected to participate in fundraising if it has not been part of their understanding of their responsibilities from the beginning. That is why the Board Resource Committee is so vital to the concept of conveying the organization's expectations from the start. The Board position descriptions should be reviewed and revised if needed by the Board Resource Committee on an annual basis. This position description then becomes part of a Board Recruitment Packet, which contains other items as well: a list of Board meeting dates, list of current Board members, organization bylaws and articles of incorporation, organization propaganda such as brochures, newsletters, and an annual report. The Board Resource Committee also needs to convey to the potential Board member the importance of Board giving for the organization as well as involvement in the organization's fundraising activities. The position description should state the number of hours and types of activities that are expected from the Board members (i.e., how many events are held by the organization at which Board attendance is mandatory or expected), number of committees, and their roles in the organization's fundraising activities. Too many organizations gloss over the fundraising role because they are afraid it will intimidate potential Board members, and then they try to introduce fundraising to the Board after they have developed a nonfundraising persona.

Board recruitment should never be a casual affair. The members of the Board Resource Committee must schedule a personal meeting with the potential candidates, and the Chief Executive Officer should always be involved in Board recruitment. The Chief Development Officer should also be a part of this meeting and should be present at orientation for new Board members, in order to convey the real importance that development and fundraising have for the organization. Often development does not have a high priority for the Board because it does not appear to be a high priority for the organization. Development staff people must be part of the senior management team, and the Chief Development Officer should report directly to the Chief Executive Officer of the organization.

The Development Committee

The Development Committee leads the Board's fundraising program. This committee, staffed by the senior development officer, will develop the long-range plan and annual work plan for the development program; assist with the process of identifying, cultivating, and soliciting donors; and lead the Board's giving program. Having a plan approved by the Development Committee will ensure that the Board will not get sidetracked with events and activities extraneous to the plan.

Often the Development Committee is divided into subcommittees such as special events, planned giving, annual giving, and Board Appeal. If the organization covers a large geographic area, it may be wise to have regional development committees that work independently and meet together once or twice a year to share ideas and ensure that each are working within the unified development plan.

Usually, unless there is a separate committee to fill this role, the Development Committee also oversees the public relations function. Because public relations is closely tied to development, these committees must have a close working relationship if they are separate. A typical position description for the Development Committee is found at the end of this chapter (see Exhibit 5.3). Like Board members, the members of the Development Committee should be carefully selected and given a full position description, outlining the expectations of committee members before they agree to serve on the committee. Time commitments and a requirement to support the organization financially should be part of this and other committee position descriptions.

Finding members of the development and other committees is often easier than finding Board members because many people may not be ready to accept the fiduciary responsibility of a Board member but want to get involved with the organization in a less responsible position. Some groups of people who may be potential Development Committee members are bankers, financial planners, attorneys, and entrepreneurs. Look for people who have served on Boards or development committees of other organizations. Recruiting a development professional from another institution, providing that organization is not a direct competitor, may be helpful. Be aware, however, that development professionals may choose not to help actively solicit donors because it could be a real or perceived conflict of interest. However, they may be helpful in planning, writing, identifying donors, and other activities. For example, a development officer from a university may be a good person to add to the Development Committee of a human service agency whose programs and donors will most likely be different and not in competition with each other.

IN THE REAL WORLD

The Importance of the
Development Committee

A human service agency had a small and ineffective Board that consisted of eight people, all of whom were parents of people served by the agency. The agency realized it needed to further develop the Board if it was going to be successful at fundraising. Knowing it would be difficult, if not impossible, to turn the Board into a power board overnight, the agency started by developing a strong Development Committee. This committee was so successful in both developing new funding streams and motivating the Board to get involved in fundraising that several members of the Development Committee were invited to serve on the Board when positions become available. This happened each year for several years, each year replenishing Development Committee members who had joined the Board with new faces on the Development Committee. Within about four years, the Board comprised more than 20 community leaders and was in a position to consider a capital campaign. Members of the Development Committee included development professionals from a university and a health care institution. Both excused themselves from active solicitation roles, but their help in identifying potential donors, introducing these prospects to the organization, and assisting with the development plan was one of the keys to the success of this organization's development program. When one of these development professionals left the area, she was replaced by another development professional from a different health care agency, who introduced several major donors to this agency. These major donors became financially supportive as well as eventually serving on the agency's Board.

Advisory Boards

Many organizations find they need a special group of volunteers who serve in a capacity of fundraising but are not part of the governing Board. This often happens in organizations whose governing Boards are more of a grassroots Board and do not have the power to fundraise from the affluent and influential. Sometimes enlisting a group of people with the cash, clout, and contacts can solve the dilemma of not having a powerful fundraising Board. A word of caution with advisory boards is that by naming them that, they will think their role is strictly to give advice. If the organization wants this group to do fundraising, then it needs to make the title clearly that of a fundraising entity, not an advisory one. It also needs to clearly communicate to the members of this group that they will not just be names on a letterhead.

Some organizations have effectively used titles such as Community Development Council, Development Board, Development Council, Committee for Philanthropy, or other similar names. This conveys the true purpose of the Board as a fundraising group. These groups sometimes serve as the Development Committee, but other times are separate entities and are different from the Development Committee in that they are not involved in the planning process, but are primarily involved in a narrowly focused area, such as major gifts or planned giving. The sole purpose of this group may be to identify, cultivate, and solicit major donors (see job description in Exhibit 5.4 at the end of this chapter).

Cyril Houle cautions that advisory boards and other auxiliary groups often run into trouble defining differences between these groups and the actual governing Board of the organization. Houle says that when auxiliary groups are used, "only one board can govern. Others must have clear-cut functions, set down in writing and understood by all." Houle further states that even though the purpose of this group may be to raise money for the organization, it must be understood by all that "if this group fails, the governing Board must still raise the money or cut the program." Houle advised that a plan for coordinating the activities of various boards, committees, and councils must be in place, especially when there are multiple entities.

IN THE REAL WORLD

Involving Community Leaders

A public library, governed by a politically appointed Board, needed to raise serious dollars because its county funding had been greatly reduced. The Library Director and one Board member, understanding that it would be important to involve more community leaders in this effort, initiated a Community Development Council. Members of the Council included people from the media, an advertising agency, a development professional, and several corporate leaders. This Council was successful in implementing several special events, an annual fund drive, and eventually a capital campaign.

Summary

The Board has a special role to play in fundraising, and its members must be carefully selected and educated about their fundraising role. Some hints to help in this process are as follows:

- Develop a position description that clearly outlines fundraising as a major role of the Board.

- Communicate this expectation from the moment a potential Board member is approached by the nonprofit for consideration by the Board.

- Have a year-round process in place to identify, cultivate, and recruit Board members.

- Provide training and education on the role of fundraising in the organization.

As in fundraising, volunteer recruitment starts with the inner circle first. The Board's role as fundraisers must be clearly defined. Then recruit those who will chair campaigns, appeals, and other committees. These leadership volunteers will then be instrumental in recruiting others to join them. Welcome all volunteers into the organization with an orientation process.

Board members play a special role in the fundraising program of any organization. The Board must be involved in establishing the mission and vision for the organization and in developing a strategic plan for reaching that vision. Board members should be involved with acknowledging and recognizing donors. Board giving is critical. Before the Board can ask anyone else for a gift for any campaign or program, there must be 100 percent participation from the Board in that program or campaign.

The Development Committee is the arm of the Board that helps plan and guide all fundraising, and this committee should lead and inspire the Board to greatness in fundraising. The initiation of a special Advisory Board, Development Council, or Committee for Philanthropy can be an effective way to involve more volunteers and can motivate and inspire Board members to become more involved in fundraising.

Further Reading

Burk, Penelope. *Donor-Centered Fundraising*. Chicago: Burk & Associates, 2003.

Center on Philanthropy at Indiana University. *Giving USA*. Indianapolis, IN: AAFRC Trust for Philanthropy, 2004.

Houle, Cyril O. *Governing Boards*. San Francisco: Jossey-Bass, 1989.

Lysakowski, Linda. *Building an Effective Board of Directors*. Alexandria, VA: Association of Fundraising Professionals, 2004.

Lysakowski, Linda. *Getting Grassroots Boards to "Move and Shake."* Charity Channel, www.charitychannel.com, 2004.

Lysakowski, Linda. *Get Rid of Your Nominating Committee*. Charity Channel, www.charitychannel.com, 2004.

Lysakowski, Linda. "What's In It for Me?" *New Directions in Philanthropy*. San Francisco: Jossey-Bass, 2003.

EXHIBIT 5.1

Board of Directors Position Description

XYZ Organization

Purpose:

To act as a voting member of the Board with full authority and responsibility to develop policies for the operation of the organization; to monitor the organization's financial health, programs, and overall performance; and to provide the Chief Executive Officer with the resources to meet the needs of those persons the organization serves.

The Full Board's Responsibilities:

- Establish policy.

- Hire and evaluate the Executive Director.

- Secure adequate funding for the organization.

- Monitor finances.

- Create and update a long-range plan for the organization.

- Select and support the organization's Board officers.

- Adopt key operating policies; approve contracts as appropriate.

Individual Board Members' Duties:

- Attend Board meetings regularly.

- Become knowledgeable about the organization.

- Come to Board meetings well prepared and well informed about issues on the agenda.

- Contribute to meetings by expressing your point of view.

- Consider other points of view, make constructive suggestions, and help the Board make decisions that benefit those persons the organization serves.

continued on the next page

- Serve on at least one committee.

- Represent the organization to individuals, the public, and other organizations in a positive and professional manner.

- Support the organization through attendance at special events and activities and *through meaningful financial contributions*.

- Assume Board leadership roles when asked.

- Keep the Executive Director informed about any concerns the community may have.

- Maintain confidentiality of Board discussion.

Rationale:

Board members set corporate policies and goals and delegate authority to the Executive Director to implement them in the day-to-day management of the organization. Individual members of the Board, however, have no authority to act independently of the full Board. When they do, it can seriously damage the organization's ability to carry out its mission, Board team spirit, and the organization's image in the community. Board members who abuse their position in this way may be disciplined or censured.

Board members are also trustees of their organization who approve an annual budget that ensures the organization can meet its financial needs. In addition, Board members monitor the overall financial health of their organization by reviewing annual reports of an auditor recommended by the Executive Director. The Executive Director retains responsibility for the day-to-day operational expenditures.

Individual Board members should attend all Board meetings and actively participate in them and serve on committees or as Board officers. Finally, Board members have the responsibility to know and fulfill their proper role as Board members and to act in the best interest of those persons the organization serves.

EXHIBIT 5.2

Board Resource Committee

XYZ Organization

Purpose:

The purpose of the Board Resource Committee is to provide quality leadership for XYZ Organization in the form of the governing Board of Directors. This will be done through the regular and systematic evaluation of the board's strengths and weaknesses, the identification of potential board members, and the ongoing training and education of board members.

Reports to: Board of Directors

Staff Representative: Executive Director

Meetings:

The Board Resource Committee will meet once a month before the regular meeting of the Board of Directors and will prepare a report to be mailed with the Board packets, at least one week before the regular Board meeting.

Terms:

The Board Resource Committee will consist of at least three and not more than five Board members, with the Executive Director serving in an advisory capacity.

Duties and Responsibilities:

- Annually prepare a Board profile form to tabulate the demographic information, and the skills and talents, of the current Board of Directors.

continued on the next page

- Determine what areas of skills and talents are needed by the organization.

- Prepare a list, with input from the entire Board and others, as required, of prospective Board members.

- Review, with the Board of Directors, the list of prospective Board members.

- Arrange for a personal interview of all prospective Board members with the Executive Director and at least one Board member.

- Assist the Executive Director in the preparation of appropriate Board recruitment materials.

- Recommend, after the initial screening and interview process, new members for the Board at the annual election of new Board members meeting, and as vacancies become open.

- Prepare, annually, a slate of nominations for officers of the Board, and present this slate to the Board at the annual election of officers meeting.

- Assist the Executive Director with Board orientation sessions for new Board members.

- Educate the Board of Directors on governance issues and the importance of Board recruitment.

- Ensure that the Board of Directors consists of an appropriately diverse representation of the community.

EXHIBIT 5.3

Development Committee

XYZ Organization

The role of the Development Committee is to work with and support the Development Department in meeting the fundraising goals for the organization. This task will be accomplished in accordance with the organization's policies and procedures and in compliance with all legal and ethical requirements for fundraising. Specific duties of the Development Committee include the following:

- Work with appropriate staff to develop a long-range and short-range development plan.
- Plan and oversee all fundraising activities of the organization.
- Contribute financially to the organization and ensure full Board participation in all campaigns and projects.
- Develop a plan to engage full board participation in the organization's development programs, including 100 percent Board contributions to the organization.
- Plan and implement training of Board in fundraising and development.
- Attend all fundraising events and encourage Board members' attendance.
- Assist with the identification, cultivation, and solicitation of major gift prospects.
- Work with or assume the duties of the public relations committee.
- Demonstrate leadership by making a financial contribution to the organization.
- Review or oversee the implementation of the public relations plan.

EXHIBIT 5.4

Advisory Council

XYZ Organization

This group serves in an advisory capacity to the Board of Directors and will consist of nonvoting members. This status removes, for the Advisory Council members, the obligations that Board members have of attending monthly meetings and participating on committees. Advisory Council members do not bear the fiduciary responsibilities of the Board of Directors and are not covered under the organization's Directors and Officers liability insurance.

Expectations of Advisory Council Members

The organization expects to profit from the acumen arising from Advisory Council members' experience, expertise, and vision of the community as a whole.

The organization will look to members of the Advisory Council for advice and assistance in supporting the financial initiatives of the organization and in offering suggestions for the essential effort of fund development.

The XYZ Organization expects that Advisory Council members will become investors in the organization by making an annual personal gift as an indication that members support the goals of the XYZ Organization and the impact it has in the community.

The Advisory Council will be consulted as needed, in whole or in part, regarding matters concerning the XYZ Organization's financial status, community involvement, membership drive, annual campaign, and other issues as they arise.

What can Advisory Council members expect from the XYZ Organization?

Advisory Council members can expect to have a direct line of communication to the Board of Directors and the Executive Director, to share their thoughts, ideas, and concerns. The President of XYZ Organization and the Executive Director will communicate in writing to the Board of Directors the essence of communication with the Advisory Council members.

If desired, Advisory Council members may request that a designee of theirs with appropriate interests may be invited to serve on a committee of the Board of Directors in order to provide the Advisory Council member with firsthand information about the operation of the organization.

The organization will value the Advisory Council member's name and prestige by publishing the Council membership on its letterhead and in other publicity about XYZ Organization.

CHAPTER 6

Training and Educating Volunteers

 After reading this chapter, you will be able to:

- Design a Board and volunteer orientation program.
- Develop a training session for volunteer solicitors.
- List the basic steps of a fundraising call.
- Design a program for ongoing volunteer fundraising education.

Now that the volunteers are recruited successfully, how do they become fully engaged in and committed to the program? It starts with a successful orientation of volunteers. Most organizations have some sort of orientation for Board members but often assume that other fundraising volunteers, because they are volunteering for perhaps a limited amount of time, as in a capital campaign, do not need to receive a formal orientation to the organization. Volunteers, however, achieve better results when they understand the work of the nonprofit and are fully committed to the organization's mission. Many organizations assume that their volunteers are busy people and therefore do not want to commit any time to becoming more familiar with the organization's operation and programs, but those organizations make a fatal mistake of saying "no" for their volunteers. (These same organizations tend to not ask for enough of a financial investment from volunteers and other donors for similar reasons.) It may be that the organization simply does not believe in itself enough to understand that others will also believe and do marvelous things if given the chance. It may be that someone, usually an uncommitted Board member or other volunteer, has misled the organization into believing that it shouldn't ask too much from volunteers. However, more Board members and other volunteers end their involvement with an organization because they aren't engaged enough than because the organization has asked too much from them.

In the Real World

Using Volunteer Talent Wisely

One Board member, a professional fundraiser, was asked to serve on the Board of a local family service agency, believing that the agency was planning to embark on new fundraising ventures and needed her assistance in setting up a development program. After a few years, it became apparent that this organization relied totally on grant funding and did not intend to ever do any other type of fundraising activities. Although the Board member felt the agency did great work and that she was filling an important role in governing the organization, she felt that her talents were not really required by this organization. Soon the Board member moved on to another organization that needed and appreciated her fundraising skills. This Board member did not leave because of any conflict, lack of faith in the organization, or because too much was demanded of her by serving on the Board, but simply because she felt she was not really contributing to the Board other than attending and participating in discussions at monthly Board meetings.

Organizations often misinterpret what motivates their volunteers, just as they do not understand what motivates their donors to give. Volunteers, like donors, want to become more involved in the organizations to which they give their time and money. In fact, most people give more to the organizations that really involve them in the organization's mission and its work. Most volunteers take their commitments seriously. Although there are the occasional social climbers and volunteers who are there because their company asked them to get involved or assigned them to the volunteer role, most volunteers have made a commitment of their time because they really care about the organization. Therefore, it stands to reason that they will want to learn more about the organization because of this passion for its mission.

Robert A. Stebbins says, "many kinds of volunteering, because they foster the acquisition and expression of a combination of special skills, knowledge and experience, can be looked on as *serious leisure*." Although many researchers, Stebbins adds, cite volunteerism as a leisure activity, many volunteers have the commitment and perseverance that goes beyond what others may look at as a way to fill time. Stebbins argues that "volunteers can simultaneously pursue their activities as serious leisure and make substantial contributions both individually and collectively to the functioning of the wider community."

Volunteers who take their role seriously will find the time to attend orientation, training sessions, and receive ongoing education in order to ensure that they can be a valuable asset to the organization. The staff must, however, be cognizant of the fact that volunteers are indeed busy people and that they do not want to feel that any of this training is a waste of their time.

Orientation

Board Orientation

As stated in an earlier chapter, Board orientation is *not* the time to discuss Board expectations; this should have been done during the recruitment process. Board orientation is the time to motivate and inspire Board members. The Chair of the

Board should lead Board orientation. Other participants will include the CEO of the organization; other Board leadership, such as the chair of the Board Resource Committee, the chair of the Development Committee, and other committee chairs as appropriate; the Chief Development Officer; and other key staff of the organization.

An effective way to motivate new Board members and get them excited about the mission is a facility tour, if it is appropriate for the organization, or a virtual tour of the organization through a video or PowerPoint slide show. For example, a caseworker in a human service agency can give a brief description of a real case on which she is working; a curator of fine art can talk about the museum collection and then take new Board members on a tour of the museum, explaining the collection; a student can talk about the education he receives at the school; a children's choir can give a brief performance; a theater group can take new Board members on a backstage tour. Whatever the mission of the organization is, it needs to be a vibrant, living mission in order to inspire Board members to do great things and become more involved in the organization.

After the new Board members are oriented to the mission and programs of the organization, the other Board members can describe their committees' work within the organization, and a particularly inspired Board member can talk about his or her involvement in the organization and why he or she is committed to this Board. The Chair of the Board is generally the best person to talk about the long-range plan for the organization, where it is headed, what is its vision, and how the Board will be involved in working toward that vision. Staff members will then have their turn to talk more specifically about the goals and activities of their departments and how Board members are expected to help achieve those goals. This is when it is critical for the Chief Development Officer to outline the Development Plan for the coming year.

The current Board, staff, or the new Board members should never take Board orientation lightly. It is the time to assure new Board members that they are welcome and needed right from the start. They will get to know their fellow

Board members better as they attend meetings and through committee work, but without a proper introduction, it is difficult to get Board members involved in the work of the organization at a meaningful level. Board members desire to be a part of something they feel passionate about. Board service is a lot like a romance: the spark needs to be ignited and then tended on an ongoing basis in order for both parties to feel like it is working.

Volunteer Orientation

Just as new Board members need a solid orientation to the organization and their role in it, so volunteer fundraisers need to be introduced to the organization in a meaningful way from the beginning. Whether the volunteer fundraisers will

TIPS & TECHNIQUES

An agenda for a Board orientation session might include the following:

Welcome	Chair of the Board
Our Mission and Values	Executive Director
A Virtual Tour of Our Programs	Department Chairs
Testimonial	Service Recipient
Our Long-Range Plan and Vision	Chair of the Board and Board Committee Chairs
Development Plan	Director of Development
Board Meetings and Operation	Chair of Board Resource Committee
Discussion	All
Optional Facility Tour	New Board Members

TIPS & TECHNIQUES

Along with Board orientation, new Board members are often assigned a Board buddy or mentor to help them get acclimated to the Board. Duties of a Board mentor include the following:

- Meeting with the new Board members to welcome them to the Board, answer any questions they have about the Board structure and organization, and explain the Board personality to the new Board members.

- Calling the new Board members to remind them of Board meetings and request their attendance and participation at the Board meeting.

- Assuring that the new Board member is appropriately assigned to a Board committee.

- Answering any questions the Board member might have about the organization.

be long-term volunteers, such as members of the Development Committee, or are accepting a short-term assignment, such as capital campaign volunteers, they need to understand and be enthusiastic about the organization's mission and vision. Volunteers will be oriented in a similar manner as the Board members, with the emphasis on their fundraising role, rather than the governance role of a Board member. The agenda and goals of the fundraising volunteer orientation are similar to those of Board orientation. Like Board members, volunteers need to be made aware of the mission and vision. The same type of facility tour and/or virtual tour should be given to fundraising volunteers in order to enable them to speak with firsthand knowledge about the mission and vision when making fundraising calls. During volunteer fundraisers' orientation, ample time should be given to explaining the case for support.

Fundraising volunteers who have been a part of developing the case will be even more effective, so ongoing education and involvement of volunteers in developing the case for support is also important. (More about this topic later.) The Chief Development Officer will play a key role in the orientation of volunteer fundraisers. This person should be prepared to discuss the case, the development plan, and the fundraising activities of the organization. Position descriptions, while discussed in detail during the recruitment process, should be reviewed during the volunteer orientation. It will be critical to assign volunteers to specific committees early on in the process. If this has not been done before orientation, committee preferences can be identified during the orientation session.

Another important facet of volunteer fundraisers' orientation is introducing them to the other volunteers with whom they will interact. For Development Committee orientation, it will be helpful to have the Board Chair attend and convey to the volunteers the importance the development function provides to the Board and the organization. In orientation for specific campaign volunteers, both the Board Chair and the Campaign Chair should attend orientation. Volunteers should also be introduced to all staff involved in the development program. Staff members should have an opportunity to introduce themselves and to tell volunteers about their role in the organization's development program. Volunteers need to have a good grasp on who does what within the organization so they have a better understanding of how the Development Office functions.

Whatever the orientation is designed to cover, remember that it is crucial to allow some time to explain the mission, vision, and values of the organization, the case for support, and the long- and short-range plans of the organization. Also be sure to allow adequate time to explain again what is needed from volunteers (i.e., time commitments required, monetary investment from volunteers), and also to discuss how the team will work to accomplish goals. And always allow time for discussion and questions from volunteers.

TIPS & TECHNIQUES

A typical agenda for Development Committee orientation might include the following:

Welcome and Introductions	Board Chair
Our Mission and Values	Executive Director
Long-Range Plan and Vision	Board Chair
Our Case for Support	Director of Development
Testimonial	Service Recipient
Our Development Plan	Development Committee Chair
The Development Office	Director of Development Development Staff
The Role of the Development Committee	Development Committee Chair
Discussion	All

The agenda for a Campaign Volunteer orientation might include the following:

Welcome and Introductions	Campaign Chair
Our Mission and Values	Board Chair & Executive Director
Testimonial	Service Recipient
Our Long-Range Plan and Vision	Board Chair
Our Campaign Plan	Director of Development
Our Case for Support	Campaign Chair
The Role of Volunteers	Consultant
Discussion	All

TIPS & TECHNIQUES

Some practical tips on arranging orientation sessions are as follows:

- Select a convenient time. Many volunteers prefer to do early-morning meetings so they can get to work right after the session.

- Fill the agenda with meaningful items, such as the long-range vision of the organization, not routine things like organizational structure and finances. These items can be provided in handouts for later review by the volunteers.

- Serve light refreshments, not a time-consuming, elaborate meal.

- Prepare all speakers in advance and set time limits for each section of the agenda in order to keep it moving quickly—typically a 1- to 1.5-hour meeting works best.

- Provide the two ingredients of making a compelling case: emotional and rational reasons why people should support the organization with their time and money.

Training Sessions

Training sessions are different from orientation. Orientation is a general introduction to the organization and to the work the volunteer will be involved in; training involves giving volunteers the tools they will need to perform the tasks required of them. *All* volunteers should receive training before they are asked to make solicitation calls. This may prove challenging for an organization that has been successful in recruiting high-powered community leaders who have done a great deal of fundraising, but experience shows that all volunteers can benefit from these sessions. One way to involve those who have been involved in fundraising for other organizations is to invite them to assist with the development of the agenda and the presentation to other volunteers, asking them to speak from their

IN THE REAL WORLD

Motivating Fundraising Volunteers

One organization, a shelter for the homeless, brought its volunteer fundraisers in for an orientation. After the orientation, this group of business leaders, who would be going out asking their peers for contributions to the shelter's annual corporate appeal, was invited to take a tour of the facilities. Most were surprised to find that the campus included not only sleeping rooms for the night but also a dining room where hot meals were served, showers, a medical and dental clinic, and a day care center. The tour was led by an employee of the shelter who had been a former guest in the shelter. While he was guiding the tour, he told these fundraising volunteers his own story about how the shelter had helped him find his own apartment and hired him to work in the shelter. When these volunteer fundraisers went out to solicit their peers, they had firsthand knowledge of the organization's mission, and the corporate appeal—the organization's first—was a huge success!

own experience about what works for them and how they have been successful in other fundraising situations.

Another tip is to not call the sessions training at all, but use a more creative and meaningful name—Strategy Session, Leadership Development Session, or some other title that more closely conveys what the organization hopes to accomplish at this session, and is not demeaning to those who feel they have done enough fundraising that they don't need "training." Much of what takes place during the training session will be strategy development (e.g., what is the right approach to make an ask, how and when to schedule an appointment). During the training session, role-playing is often an effective way of working with those who are new to the fundraising arena; however, more experienced fundraisers usually prefer sharing what has been effective for them. A good strategy that combines these two approaches is to have a scenario role-played by two experienced fundraisers and then have the other volunteers practice some of the approaches used by the pros with each other, taking turns being the asker and the prospective donor.

It is important to have a leader who has the ability to train volunteers at the level at which they will be most comfortable. In many cases, if the organization is working with a consultant, that person will train volunteers, with assistance from the development staff. If the organization is not working with a consultant, it will need to have experienced development staff members who can work well with volunteers and provide them the training they will need to be successful. Sometimes bringing in a volunteer from another organization that has been successful in fundraising or using one of the more experienced

IN THE REAL WORLD

Role Playing

One organization was conducting a capital campaign and was ready to launch its business appeal. Most of the volunteers had limited experience, having done some fundraising but not having attended any formal fundraising training. One volunteer, however, clearly thought of himself as having had enough experience that he didn't need any training, and he was the perceived, if not the actual, leader of the group of volunteers. In order to involve this volunteer in the training, the facilitator asked a question early on about how many people really enjoyed fundraising, knowing that this volunteer would most likely be the only one to raise his hand. When he did exactly that, the facilitator invited him to do a role-playing scenario with her for the rest of the group. The facilitator was not an easy ask for the volunteer, so he had to use all of his fundraising experience and expertise before she made a commitment. After this session, the volunteers were invited to practice with each other, using tips gained during the role-playing session.

fundraising volunteers the organization has recruited, can work well. There are tools available for training volunteers in making an ask. For example, *Board-Source* has an excellent video, *Speaking of Money*, designed for Board members who need to understand their role in fundraising. This video walks volunteers through the process of fundraising and can help them feel more comfortable with the solicitation process.

The role of the trainer is to help the volunteers understand the philanthropic process. Doug Lawson describes fundraising as the bringing together of a "joyful giver, a grateful recipient, and an artful asker." The trainer needs to convey the importance and the excitement of helping someone make a philanthropic gift, to help others feel the joy of giving. Few people wake up each morning saying, "I can't wait to go ask someone for money for my favorite charity!" Many volunteers view fundraising as an unpleasant task, one to be done as quickly and quietly as possible. However, the joy of giving is something that all volunteers have probably felt themselves, and if they are motivated and properly trained, they can help others feel that same joy.

Sometimes, because of the geographic location and/or busy schedules of volunteers, organizations feel they cannot effectively do training for fundraising volunteers. It is important, however, to get volunteers together for these sessions before they go out and make calls. Some organizations use multiple sessions or meet with volunteers individually to review strategy and provide tips on making solicitations. Virtual training sessions have even been used by some organizations, putting the training information on a CD and mailing it to volunteers, or doing a training session by phone and e-mail.

Fundraising is a science and an art, and it can be learned. The trainer must understand adult learning styles and know the importance of getting the volunteers involved in the training process. An artful trainer will ask volunteers to recall their own feelings about giving, perhaps inviting them to stop and think about the last time they made a gift to a charity and to tell the rest of the volunteers what compelled them to make that gift. Volunteers might also be asked to reflect on why

Virtual Training

One organization, which was running a statewide campaign, had a challenge in getting its volunteers together because many of them had a five- to six-hour drive to get to the organization's headquarters. A virtual training session was scheduled in which the consultant, in a different state, led the volunteers through a training session by phone. A PowerPoint presentation had been sent to the participants in advance, along with a list of solicitation tips and a list of the prospects, which had been developed in a previous virtual strategy session. Although the lack of face-to-face interaction was a slight deterrent to the process, all of the volunteers heard the same training tips and had ample time to ask questions.

they do not make gifts to some solicitors or why they stopped supporting an organization financially. These techniques help the volunteer understand the philanthropic process. For those who are fairly new to fundraising, it also helps to provide them with some basic information about giving and asking.

For instance, the training might include sharing with volunteers the Giving USA charts mentioned previously about how much giving is from individuals and trends in corporate and foundation giving, if they will be soliciting corporations or foundations. It is also helpful to share with them the return on investment of personal solicitation compared to other fundraising techniques, such as direct mail and telephone fundraising, and to stress the importance of building relationships. After all, the three keywords in fundraising are Relationships, Relationships, and Relationships. Volunteers need to know that even if they didn't get a commitment from the prospect, the call was not necessarily a failure if it helped forge or further develop a relationship between the organization and the prospective donor.

The effective trainer will also emphasize how important the volunteers' role as fundraisers is for the organization. It is good to do a quick review of the development process so the volunteers know where they fit into the overall program. For example, volunteers in the small business division of a capital campaign should be aware of the progress of the leadership and major gifts team and that there will be a student phone-a-thon and a direct mail appeal following their effort.

Training for the solicitation process is crucial for fundraising volunteers. Many Board members and volunteers want to help the organizations to which they are committed, but they simply don't know how to do fundraising. Training must always be done with the end result of taking the fear out of fundraising for these volunteers. Teaching them the art of the ask is important, not only for the organization but also to help the volunteers grow personally. Volunteers, after all, are seeking to not only give but also to receive some satisfaction from the work they do for nonprofits. An inspirational training session can do wonders to boost the morale of volunteers, provide them with the skills they need to be successful fundraisers, and build a cohesive bond between the volunteers and the organization.

 TIPS & TECHNIQUES

A typical agenda for volunteer training might include the following:

Welcome and Introduction	Campaign Chair
Remarks	Board Chair, Executive Director
The Case for Support and Campaign Materials to be used in the solicitation process	Development, Director
The Solicitation Process	Consultant
Scheduling the Appointment	
Making the Ask	
Follow-Up	
Case Studies in Asking	Volunteers

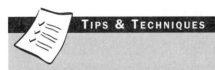

TIPS & TECHNIQUES

Items to be covered during the solicitation training session include the following:

- Volunteers must always make their own gifts first.
- The volunteer solicitation team needs to be carefully chosen.
- Volunteers must be able to articulate the case.
- Volunteers will be given donor history and other pertinent information.
- The solicitation team needs to rehearse in advance but be prepared for the unexpected.
- Always have a targeted ask amount in mind for each prospect that will be visited.
- Setting the appointment is often the hardest part of the ask.
- Volunteers must be prepared to share with the prospective donor that they have already made a gift themselves.
- Volunteers should be prepared to answer questions the prospect might have or to get back to them with answers if they cannot answer questions.
- Once the case has been explained and the level of interest has been determined, it is usually time to make the ask.
- Always ask for a specific amount of money.
- Once the ask is on the table, the volunteers should remain quiet.
- Be prepared for the fact that in most major gift solicitations, the prospect is not ready to make a decision at the time of the first ask.
- Do not simply leave a pledge card to be completed and returned by the prospect.
- Always follow up with donor prospect visits.

These points are elaborated on in the following sections.

Volunteers Must Always Make Their Own Gifts First

The fundraising volunteers are part of the family of the organization, those closest to it, and they will be solicited before they call on others to make a gift. It is crucial that all volunteers understand that they must make a gift before they can successfully solicit others. This is often one of the reasons to have an outside trainer involved; it is easy for a consultant, as an outsider, to tell volunteers how important their financial commitment is, and sometimes more difficult for a staff person to say this to volunteers. When making solicitations, volunteers are most successful when they can say to prospective donors, "I know you share my commitment to (feeding the homeless, making our community a safer place for our children, promoting a rich culture through art and music, or whatever the mission is), and I would like you to join me in making an investment in this organization."

The Volunteer Solicitation Team Needs To Be Carefully Chosen

Team solicitation is always more successful than one-on-one solicitation. Having two people make a call shows the donors they are important to the organization and that it is a well-planned approach. It is best to have two people making the ask, but a word of caution in using too large a team: More than two people can be intimidating to the prospective donor. One organization sent five people to talk with a prospective donor in his office, resulting in a smaller gift than the organization had targeted for this prospect. One of the advantages of using the team approach is that most volunteers feel more secure when they are in a team. They may be concerned that they will forget an important point in the asking process, and having another person with them will help alleviate these fears. Often, one member of the team is a good asker and the other is a good listener. Listening is often 90 percent of a successful call, and asking only 10 percent, so assure the volunteers who may be shy about asking that their involvement in the call is equally important if they can pick up on something the prospective donors said that may be the pivotal point in getting the donors to give.

Generally, the best combination is a volunteer and staff member together calling on a prospective donor. When calling on chief executives, the volunteers should include the chief executive officer of the nonprofit organization and a volunteer who is also in a chief executive position. Peer-to-peer solicitation is a must in major gift fundraising. Some organizations feel that if the development staff is skilled in fundraising, they should make the calls themselves; however, there is no underestimating the ask made by someone who is on an equal standing with the prospective donor financially, socially, and professionally.

Volunteers Must Be Able to Articulate the Case

As already discussed, when volunteers have been involved in the development of the case, or at the very least have gone through orientation and training that includes an exciting interpretation of the case, they will be well versed about the mission and vision of the organization and should be able to articulate the case to prospective donors. Providing the volunteers with the proper training and building enthusiasm and excitement in them about the project they are asking donors to fund is the first step in ensuring that they have the desire and ability to make a compelling case. The second step is involving them in role-playing at the training so volunteers will feel comfortable in presenting the case to prospective donors. The volunteer who is having difficulty in presenting the case can be teamed with another volunteer who is more fluent is his or her ability to articulate the case. Team solicitation helps ensure that at least one of the askers is comfortable in presenting the case. Often the staff person takes the lead role in this part of the solicitation call, leaving the actual ask to the volunteer, but volunteers should also feel comfortable with explaining the needs of the organization.

Volunteers Will Be Given Donor History and Other Pertinent Information

It is important for staff members to provide information about the potential donors with whom they will be meeting as well as appropriate fundraising materials to be shared with the prospect. However, donor information is not to be shared lightly, and an anonymous gift should never be revealed to *anyone* outside the Development Office or the organization's leadership. However, if the donor's giving history with the organization is public record, it should be shared with volunteers who will be calling on this donor. Nothing is more embarrassing for a volunteer than to make an ask not knowing what the donor's previous involvement with the organization has been. Not only donor history but also information the organization may have about the prospective donor's interest and involvement with the organization or with similar organizations will be helpful when making a solicitation call and should be shared with the volunteers as appropriate. Similarly, information garnered through research, as long as it has been obtained legally and ethically, should be shared with the volunteers when appropriate to do so. For further information about the ethical issues involved with donor records and research, see the ethical codes of the Association of Fundraising Professionals and the Association of Professional Research for Advancement.

Volunteers also need to be supplied with appropriate materials to make a call. The case statement, a personalized proposal, pledge cards or letter of intent, and fact sheets are some of the tools typically used in solicitation calls. Sometimes a video may be shown or left with the prospect or a PowerPoint presentation viewed on a laptop computer. A question-and-answer sheet is often produced that addresses anticipated questions the prospect may have about the project. A list of solicitation tips will also serve as a reminder of topics covered during the training session and can be referred to by volunteers just before making the solicitation call. Some unanticipated issues will always arise, but the more tools that can provide information for the volunteers, the more confident they will be when making calls.

The Solicitation Team Needs to Rehearse in Advance but Be Prepared for the Unexpected

Armed with the appropriate information and materials, the solicitation team must meet before the day of the solicitation visit and prepare for their call. Some things to be addressed in this meeting include (1) Who will make the initial call to schedule the appointment? (2) What dates will work for the team and the prospective donor? (3) Where will the meeting take place? (4) Will the team meet there or drive together to the prospect's home or office? (5) If the meeting involves a meal, who will pick up the check? (6) Who will start the conversation? (7) Who will present the case? (8) Who will make the ask? (9) Who will close the meeting and schedule the follow-up meeting? (10) When will the team get together to debrief on the meeting? and (11) Who will report the results to the organization?

Even with a full dress rehearsal, sometimes the unexpected happens: the prospect has a last-minute emergency and needs to cut the meeting short; the prospect is unhappy with the organization and no one knew it; the prospect has already thought about the amount of his or her gift and it is nowhere near the amount being asked; the prospect is interested in another facet of the organization's program than he or she is being asked to fund. All of these situations and many more are possibilities and require contingency plans, which is why the debriefing with volunteers and staff is critical.

Always Have a Targeted Ask Amount in Mind for Each Prospect That Will Be Visited

Soliciting donors by asking them to consider a gift of any size is *not* an effective way to make a call. Volunteers often shy away from asking for a specific amount if they don't feel comfortable with this process. Volunteers who will be making the call should be involved with establishing the proper ask amount. An important part of the strategy meetings held before the training session is the establishment of an ask amount for every prospect. Although sometimes this amount may be found to be too high or too low, it is a starting point for discussion. During the strategy session, volunteers should discuss the donor's ability and propensity to give in order to arrive at a reasonable ask amount. It is never an exact science, but the more research and discussion of ask amounts that takes place before the call, the more successful the volunteers will be at making the ask. When the prospect is considering a smaller gift, volunteers should be trained in the options that will be available to bring the donor up to the ask amount that has been determined.

Setting the Appointment Is Often the Hardest Part of the Ask

Once the volunteers get the appointment, it is almost certain the donor is considering a gift. One of the key strategies is to determine who is the best person to call the prospect for an appointment. It should be the person who has the best chance of getting to meet with the prospective donor. This is why the strategy session and the volunteer team rehearsal are important steps in the process. Volunteers should not try to be vague with the prospect about the purpose of the visit. They need to contact the person, requesting a meeting of 30 to 45 minutes to discuss an exciting opportunity for the prospect to be a part of the organization's mission and vision. Often the prospect will want to talk longer and may have a lot of questions, so the meeting will most likely run over that time, but the volunteers must be considerate of the prospect's time. Volunteers should also be aware of the fact that solicitations are usually best done on the prospect's home turf—his or her office or home is the best location for an ask. Inviting the prospect to the organization's facility is a good cultivation strategy, but in most cases, the prospect will feel more comfortable when being solicited in his or her own surroundings. This option also gives the volunteers an opportunity to observe the prospect's surroundings, gaining valuable insight into the prospect's financial situation and interests. (See Exhibit 6.1 at the end of this chapter for a useful contact report form.)

Volunteers Must Be Prepared to Share with the Prospective Donor That They Have Already Made a Gift Themselves

Generally, this gift will be in the same range as the prospective donor that is being asked. This is one reason why volunteers make such good askers, because they have already made a similar commitment and can ask others to join them in their investment in the organization. It is not necessary for the volunteers to share the amount of their gift with the prospective donors, although often volunteers who have a good relationship with the prospective donor may feel comfortable doing this. What is important, however, is that the volunteers can tell the prospective donors that they have made a commitment of their own when inviting others to join them in this commitment. Volunteers who haven't made their own commitment should be invited and required to do so before they schedule their appointments.

Volunteers Should Be Prepared to Answer Questions the Prospect Might Have

The fact sheet and case for support usually address most questions that prospective donors will have about the project, and someone on the solicitation team should have a good knowledge of the organization and the project and be able to answer almost any questions that might arise. However, there are occasionally questions that cannot be answered on the spot. In general, the larger a gift being considered, the more questions the prospective donor will have. The volunteers must be prepared to answer questions or to assure the prospective donor that they will get back to them with answers if they do not have them now. Volunteers must be trained to complete a call report (see Exhibit 6.1 at the end of this chapter) for all of the calls they make. This call report, among other things, should list any questions the prospect might have. In most cases, it is suggested that the volunteers who made the call follow up with the prospects with answers to their questions; however, sometimes it is good to have a specialist within the organization make a follow-up call. For example, a prospective donor may have detailed questions about a project budget and may need to speak with the Chief Financial Officer of the organization. Or, the donor may have a question about a program that requires information from the staff person in charge of that program.

Once the Case Has Been Explained and the Level of Interest Has Been Determined, It Is Usually Time to Make the Ask

The right time to make the ask is one of the trickiest parts of the solicitation process. Sometimes a volunteer will want to make the ask prematurely and get it over with. Other times, volunteers may be reluctant to make the ask at the proper time, waiting for everything to be perfect. Other times, it is difficult for the volunteers to assess the prospect's readiness to be solicited. Sometimes the prospect will give clear signals or make a direct statement like, "So how much are you expecting me to give?" Even a statement like this may not mean the prospect is really ready to be asked. If the prospective donors seem eager to get the meeting over with, it may be best to suggest a follow-up meeting after they have had time to review the case for support. If the questions the prospects have seem to preclude their making a decision at this time, again it is best to suggest another meeting after the volunteer has the answers for the prospects' questions. If the prospects are visibly excited about the project and want to know how they can be involved, it is probably the right time to make the ask. This is where the observant listener comes into play and can give the signal to the asker that now is the time.

Always Ask for a Specific Amount of Money

Once the amount has been determined with the volunteer input, it should be easy for the volunteer to ask for that amount. However, volunteers often have trouble getting out the ask and stumble with this part of the meeting. A good technique is to ask the prospect to "consider a gift in the range of $10,000" (or whatever the predetermined ask amount is). Asking in this manner gives the prospective donors the option to suggest another amount if this is not an appropriate request and to consider other amounts, without feeling that they have not met expectations. Although the phrase "in the range of" was used in this approach, an actual range is not recommended. Donors will almost always choose the lower end of the range when asked for a gift in the range of $5,000 to $10,000. One thing is important for volunteers to know: no one is ever insulted by being asked for too much, but a prospect *can* be insulted by not being asked for enough. Once the organization has done its homework and the prospective donors are properly motivated and approached, most will want to be a part of the larger vision. So aim high in the ask, and use that figure as the starting point in the conversation that will eventually arrive at a signed pledge card.

 IN THE REAL WORLD

Ask High

One donor, having made annual gifts of between $100 and $250 to an organization, received a phone call during the annual phone-a-thon, asking her for a $25 gift. The donor was surprised that she was asked for such a small amount and wondered if the caller had even bothered to look up her past giving history. She was, in fact, insulted that the organization had targeted her at such a low level. Her gift to the annual fund that year was $25—exactly what the organization had asked for! Imagine what could have happened if this donor had been a $1 million or even a $25,000 donor?

Once the Ask Is on the Table, Volunteers Should Remain Quiet

This is usually the most difficult part of the ask for most volunteers, but it is critical not to answer for the donor or to jump in and try to justify the ask; give the donor time to think and react. Too often a volunteer will make the ask at the right time, in the right way, and for the right amount, but then mistakenly take the prospect's momentary silence as a "no," and immediately jump in with a statement like, "Well, if that is too much, any size gift will be appreciated." Or "Well, if you can't do that amount, what amount might you consider?" Volunteers should be trained to understand that "silence is golden," and to allow the prospective donor time to think about the request and respond to it. Once the donor responds, it will be a yes, a no, or a maybe. Celebrate the positive responses, learn from the negative ones, and be aware that most of the time, a "no" is not a "no forever." Perhaps it is "no, not now," a "no, not that amount," or a "no, not that project." Effective volunteers will learn how to probe for the real answer and deal with it.

Be Prepared for the Fact That in Most Major Gift Asks, the Prospect Is Not Ready to Make a Decision at the Time of the First Ask

Usually the prospective donor will need to consult advisors, talk it over with a significant other, or think and/or pray about it for a while, so a return visit will need to be scheduled. A general rule of thumb is that if the major donor prospect does make a pledge during the first visit, he or she was probably not asked for enough. In most cases, the donor who needs to think about his or her decision, to consult with others, or to have questions answered is considering a much larger gift than would result if a decision were made on the spot. The key for volunteers will be to determine what is holding the prospect back from making a gift. If the timing is bad, they should explore options for making a commitment with deferred payments, perhaps even a planned gift. If the project is not exciting for the prospective donor, perhaps there is some other program this organization may ask the prospect to fund. If the amount is too high, explore options such as pledge payments, matching gifts, or group or family gifts.

Do Not Simply Leave a Pledge Card to Be Completed and Returned by the Prospect

Occasionally, prospective donors will ask the volunteers to just leave a pledge card and they will mail it in to the organization. This approach is *not* recommended because it generally results in no gift at all or a gift at a lower level than has been targeted for this prospect. More important, offering to leave a pledge card implies to the prospect that this is not an important ask. The volunteers should stress to the prospective donor that because this is such an important project and because the prospect's involvement is critical to the campaign's success, they will be happy to come back again after the prospect has had sufficient time to think about the request, consult advisors, or have questions answered. Before leaving the donor prospect, the volunteer team must be sure to establish a next meeting time and place for the meeting. Sometimes the prospect needs more cultivation, and this should be noted by the volunteers on the call report and in the debriefing meeting.

Always Follow up with Donor Prospect Visits

Send a personal thank-you note, call the prospects to thank them for their time, and be sure to get them any requested information in a timely manner. Also, volunteers need to complete their call reports and report to the staff and/or volunteer leadership the results of their calls in a timely manner. All prospects should be thanked regardless of the outcome of the visit. Debriefing with staff and the volunteer team should take place soon after the call to evaluate the results. What went wrong? What went right? Is the donor ready to make a commitment at the next visit? Does he or she need more cultivation? More information? The debriefing is an important part of the moves management process.

Report Meetings

After solicitation calls have been completed, it is important to schedule regular report meetings with volunteers to report results and share successful and unsuccessful solicitation calls. Even though this means additional meetings for volunteers to attend, it will be important to track progress and equally important to give volunteers opportunities to share success stories as well as ask for advice when calls do not go well. In most campaigns, report meetings are scheduled at least monthly, giving volunteers an opportunity to share with each other what has worked and not worked. Regular report meetings also tend to spur movement in those who have procrastinated in making their calls. Volunteers should be told up front that they will be expected to attend regular report meetings during the time they will be involved in making solicitation calls. In cases where the volunteers are part of a team, the team should have regular report meetings among themselves, and the team leader will then report team results at team leader report meetings.

Ongoing Education for Volunteers

The fact that fundraising volunteers have been oriented and trained to make the calls doesn't mean they do not need ongoing education and support. Particularly with long-term fundraising volunteers, such as members of the Development Committee, ongoing education is critical. The organization will often change focus during the tenure of Development Committee members; for example, the organization may enter into a capital campaign or initiate a planned giving program, and volunteers will need to be educated by specialists in these areas. Or, an organization that has primarily used volunteers only for special events may need to bring in a consultant to help educate the Board and other volunteers on making personal solicitations. Furthermore, an organization, while remaining true to its mission, may change the focus of its programs, and fundraising volunteers will need to be made aware of these new services and programs.

The organization should assess volunteer educational needs annually and prepare a plan to educate volunteers in the areas needed. Board members in particular will need to be kept up to date on significant changes within the organization and new trends in fundraising. A classic example might be education of Board members on a new e-philanthropy program the organization has initiated. Or, the case for support of an organization will be adjusted in light of a new expansion of programming to serve a new constituency or to move into a new program area. The Board and other volunteers should be involved in developing a new case for support based on these new directions. Those volunteers who will be involved in soliciting donations will need, at the very least, to be made aware of the current case. For many organizations, the case may change annually as new areas are emphasized, and volunteer fundraisers should be made aware of the updated case annually.

One way to involve the Board and other volunteers in the development of the case would be to conduct strategic interviews with Board members and other volunteers. During the interviews, ask them about the elements of the organization's program that they feel are the most compelling for donors, get them to provide input into budgets for program areas, solicit their help in developing giving levels and named giving opportunities, and invite them to assess the relevance of the program in light of the organization's mission and vision and community needs. Another approach is to bring a group of Board members and other fundraising volunteers together for a case development planning session. Working as a group, these volunteers will review the mission and vision to ensure that they are still relevant and appropriate for the organization and meet community needs. Working in small groups and then coming together as a whole, the volunteers will determine which areas of the organization's history should be highlighted in the case, without making the case look like a laundry list of dates that are not of interest to most readers. The group can then be again divided into smaller groups to develop or prioritize items for which the organization will be asking for contributions. After the entire group assesses the work of the small groups and establishes priority items, they can then help develop key phrases that will resonate with donors and make the case compelling on both a rational and an emotional level. Involving volunteers in the case development helps the organization develop a case that is written from the donor's point of view, and at the same time, educates volunteers about the organization, its program, and needs. It involves volunteers in a meaningful way in the case, so that when they are asked to articulate that case to potential donors, they are able to do so in a compelling way.

Remember that when preparing for a capital campaign, Board and volunteers will need to be educated in several areas; the Board in particular will need to know if the organization is ready for a campaign, and the Board should bring in an expert to discuss the essential ingredients of capital campaigns and participate in assessing the organization's readiness for a campaign. Once a planning study has been completed and the organization is ready to launch a campaign, Board members should be the first group to be educated in the psychology and techniques of campaigning. Board members will need to be involved in selecting the right volunteers to join the campaign cabinet, so they will need to be educated in the role of volunteers in a campaign. Once the campaign cabinet is established, those volunteers will also need education in specific areas. For example, the Leadership and/or Major Gifts Committee members will need to be educated in planned giving and how it relates to the campaign, donor solicitation strategies, and so on. Other cabinet members may need education in the specific areas in which their committee will function.

As the organization prepares to get involved in planned giving, some good educational opportunities include bringing in an estate attorney to educate the Board first and then the Development Committee about the various techniques used in estate planning that can benefit the organization. Insurance agents specializing in charitable instruments, financial planners, trust officers of banks, and accountants can all provide a different focus on planned giving that can be helpful to the organization. Remember that volunteers and Board members, like staff, do not have to be experts in all of the intricacies of planned gifts. What they need to know is that these instruments exist and that they can benefit the donor and the organization, and how to initiate a conversation with potential donors about planned giving. Any education about capital campaigns, planned giving, or any type of fundraising must include teaching Board members and volunteers that they must make their own gift first before asking others.

Further Reading

Lawson, Doug. *Give to Live*. New York: Abingdon Press, 1995.

Stebbins, Robert A. "Volunteering: A Serious Leisure Perspective." *Nonprofit and Voluntary Sector Quarterly*, Volume 25, Number 2, June 1996.

BoardSource *Speaking of Money* video.

Association of Fundraising Professionals (AFP) Code of Ethical Principles and Standards of Professional Practice.

Association of Prospect Research for Advancement (APRA) Statement of Ethics.

EXHIBIT 6.1

Confidential Contact Report

XYZ Organization

Contact Name:	Date of Contact:

Volunteer and/or Staff Member:

Type of Call: ☐ Personal Visit ☐ Telephone ☐ Letter

Business Address:	Home Address:
E-mail	E-mail
Website	Website
Telephone: ( )	Telephone: ( )
Fax: ( )	Fax: ( )

CONTACT SUMMARY: Information obtained should be as comprehensive as possible (i.e., indications of political or religious preference, remarks about family, hobbies, community interest, state of health, quality of reception, personality traits, degree of familiarity with organization, attitudes, etc.) (*Please write clearly.*)

Date of Next Action Step:

Next Step:

☐ Send Literature   ☐ In-Person Visit   ☐ Solicit

☐ Send Letter   ☐ No Further Action   ☐ Post-solicit

☐ Phone Call   ☐ Cultivate   ☐ Re-solicit

☐ Other

REQUEST AMOUNT:	STEP: RECOMMEND AFTER CALL:	CAPABILITY:
Suggested:_____	☐ Possible Prospect/Needs Research	☐ $1 million plus
Actual: _____	☐ Capability Determined/Research Done	☐ $500, 000–$999,999
	☐ Cultivation/Solicitor Assignment Made	☐ $250,000–$499,999
PRIORITY:	☐ Solicited/No Decision	☐ $100,000–$249,999
RECOMMENDATION AFTER CALL	☐ Solicited/Favorable	☐ $50,000–$99,999
☐ Close within 30 days	☐ Solicited/Decline	☐ $25,000–$49,999
☐ Close within 90 days	LEVEL OF INTEREST:	☐ $5,000–$24,999
☐ Close within 180 days	☐ High ☐ Moderate	
☐ Close within 1 year	☐ Low ☐ Uncertain	

Areas of Interest:

Questions about Project:

135

CHAPTER 7

Staff and Volunteers Working Together to Raise Money

 After reading this chapter, you will be able to:

- List the expectations of fundraising volunteers.
- Design a volunteer recognition program.
- Develop a strategy to recruit corporate volunteers.

One experienced fundraiser says,

> I have found the key to volunteer success is to have a staff member partner along with the volunteer, to be sure the volunteer is well trained and to be sure that the first couple of calls are yeses for confidence building; the volunteer's confidence coupled with the passion for the organization are unbeatable qualities going forward; also it is helpful if volunteers, especially board members, have had a part in developing "the Case."

As stated earlier, a staff member and a volunteer are generally the ideal solicitation team, but volunteers and staff need to learn to work together effectively in order to be successful at fundraising. First, they need to understand each other's expectations. In an article in *Contributions*, Jarene Frances Lee tells staff they need to prepare for working with volunteers in five ways: (1) defining responsibilities and authority, (2) developing a training plan, (3) preparing the workplace, (4) relationships and communications, and (5) feedback and recognition. Although Lee's article is primarily focused on program volunteers, her advice can easily be transferred to fundraising volunteers.

Assessing volunteer needs and preparing position descriptions has already been discussed. However, another important point made by Lee is that authority needs to be defined: Do the volunteers have the authority to spend the organization's money, make policy decisions, and set priorities for their work? Some basic things should be outlined in writing, covering areas such as: If the volunteers take a prospective donor out for lunch or dinner, will the organization reimburse them? Volunteers also need to be aware of limits on their authority. For example, the Gift Acceptance Policies must be developed by staff and approved by the Board, and only the Board has the authority to make policy decisions. A volunteer should not have the authority to accept gifts outside the scope of Board-approved policy. Providing limits on volunteers' authority in writing at the beginning of their involvement with the organization can save a great deal of embarrassment later, and perhaps hard feelings or losing the volunteers altogether.

Lee further says that one of the greatest mistakes organizations make is not devoting enough time to training new volunteers. Even if fundraising volunteers have been involved in fundraising activities for other organizations, it cannot be assumed that they have received adequate training. The training process for fundraising volunteers not only equips them with the skills they need, but also helps bond them to the organization and helps them develop a passion for the organization's mission. Fundraising volunteers, in fact, may require more training than program volunteers because they will be interacting with some of the most important people with whom the organization relates—donors.

Lee's article talks about preparing a safe, secure, and comfortable workplace for volunteers who work in the organization's facility. In most cases, fundraising volunteers will be doing their work outside of the organization's facility, but the environment of the facility can still have a great impact on these volunteers. Volunteers will be coming into the office for meetings, orientations, to visit staff, and so on. Do the receptionist and other staff members greet volunteers with dignity and respect? Is the Development Office located in a convenient part of the facility, and does its appearance look professional? Do staff members dress and act professionally? All of these things can help build the confidence the fundraising volunteers place in the organization. Remember that fundraising is everyone's job in a nonprofit organization. Development staff should develop a good working relationship with all of the other departments in the organization and provide an orientation to other departments about the work of development and the importance of maintaining a professional environment, especially when dealing with volunteers from the business world. These volunteers will not accept unprofessional behavior.

Lee talks about the importance of building lasting relationships with volunteers and keeping open lines of communication between staff and volunteers and among volunteers. This is especially critical in working with fundraising volunteers. Give volunteers an opportunity to get to know each other. Fundraising volunteers are often motivated by the ability to network with other community leaders. Some will want to know who else is involved before they come on board. Although organizations do not want to recruit volunteers who are only interested in networking opportunities, they must recognize that this can be an extra benefit to volunteers. Many great business contacts have been made through volunteer work. Relationships with staff can also be a motivating factor for volunteers. If the relationship with staff is solid, the volunteers will be more likely to stay involved with an organization. This does not mean the staff has to be best friends with every volunteer. However, staff can help build good relationships by following some common courtesy rules: (1) always return phone calls and e-mails from volunteers in a timely manner; (2) ask the volunteers how they wish to be addressed in public (e.g., Doctor Johnson or Harry); and (3) ask volunteers which method of communication they prefer (e.g., e-mail, phone, cell phone, office or home mail), and use that method to communicate with them.

Providing a complete list of volunteers who will be working on a project together with contact information helps volunteers communicate with each other in the preferred manner as well. However, be sure not to give out personal information that the volunteers may not want shared with other volunteers. As with building relationships with donors, small things can be important. The staff should be observant and make notes in the volunteer files about things like personal information, preferences, and so on. Sending volunteers a birthday card or a note of congratulations on a job promotion, knowing a person's dietary restrictions and assuring that special meals are provided for that volunteer at meetings, and other such thoughtful things can go a long way toward building long-lasting relationships with volunteers just as they do with donors.

Feedback and recognition are the final keys to success, Lee asserts. Although acknowledgment and feedback need to happen often, recognition should be a more formal process. Staff members need to remember to say thank you to fundraising volunteers and give them positive feedback on both their successes and their failures. The report meetings discussed in the last chapter provide a good opportunity to praise and recognize volunteers who have had successful calls, but also provide an opportunity to coach volunteers and help the entire group learn from unsuccessful calls. Recognition provides a good incentive for many volunteers. Recognition can be in the form of press coverage after a successful campaign has been completed, a listing in the annual report and/or the local newspaper of all the fundraising volunteers who helped the organization achieve its goals, an article in the quarterly newsletter about a volunteer or team of volunteers that have been successful in reaching new donors, or a gift presented at the victory celebration after a campaign is completed. Most volunteers especially appreciate gifts with a connection to the volunteer's personal interests or ones that relate to the organization's mission.

Volunteer Recognition

Two examples of recognition gifts that proved to be effective ways of thanking a volunteer are as follows:

A small private college, at the end of its annual corporate appeal, thanked volunteers who had been involved in several ways. First, they placed an ad in the local newspaper listing all of the volunteers. The president of the school sent a personal note to each volunteer. Also, during the appeal, several gifts in kind were received from companies that chose not to give cash gifts (e.g., gift certificates from restaurants and theaters, candy, wine, and other items). These gifts were used as prizes for the team that gathered the highest number of pledges, the individual who raised the most money, the team that completed its calls first, and so on. After several years of doing this, the prizes, although not high in dollar value, got to be coveted forms of recognition, especially for those with a competitive nature. The Chair of the Committee received a dinner gift certificate at his favorite restaurant and a jacket with the college logo, both gifts that were meaningful to the volunteer. The college also ran an article about this volunteer in the quarterly magazine.

Another organization, when recognizing its past chairs, selected unique gifts that they knew the volunteers would treasure for many years. One past chair who had a great love for trees and was a high-achieving business owner received a framed photograph of a person standing on a mountaintop under a windswept tree, with a poem about achievement and a plaque engraved with the organization's appreciation for her service. The gift was meaningful to this volunteer and prompted her to remain involved with the organization long after her Board service ended.

Many organizations simply lose touch with volunteers once their current service has ended, especially Board members. Board members and other volunteers should remain on mailing lists, be invited to special events, and be called on for advice long after their volunteer service has ended. An organization that has an annual special event can keep former members of the committee involved by asking former chairs to serve as advisors to the committees in following years. A Past President's Council comprising former Board presidents can be an effective way of keeping valued volunteers involved. Sometimes organizations move high-achieving volunteers or Board members into an emeritus status, keeping them involved in an advisory capacity. Often the volunteers appreciate this form of recognition and involvement because their time commitment is lessened and the level of their obligation as a volunteer is lowered. Often they will keep the organization in mind for future donations and are willing to make connections with their contacts, introducing them to staff or new volunteers, who will continue building the relationship between the donors and the organization. Being aware of the things that motivate volunteers will help staff maintain good relationships with their volunteers.

 TIPS & TECHNIQUES

Stebbins cites nine personal rewards of volunteerism:

- Personal enrichment.
- Self-actualization.
- Self-expression.
- Self-image.
- Self-gratification.
- Recreation.
- Financial return.

And two social rewards:

- Social attraction (associating with clients and other volunteers, participation in the social world of the activity).
- Group accomplishment.

In the article previously quoted, Stebbins says that often "a volunteer board member might not always feel like attending board meetings, might occasionally have his or her ideas rejected when at the meetings, and might be asked to perform some disagreeable tasks but still regard this activity as satisfying—as leisure—because of certain powerful rewards it offers."

Many volunteers feel that their volunteer experiences will enhance them personally. If volunteers are given the opportunity to learn a new skill, especially one that is desired by other nonprofits—as fundraising is—they feel they are receiving something in return for the time and effort they are offering the nonprofit. For many volunteers, community service is part of the self-actualization process; in order to feel their life is complete, they need to give back in some way, and because most organizations desperately need fundraising volunteers, the volunteers who can contribute to society in this manner will feel fulfilled. For others, fundraising may be a form of self-expression, particularly when they associate closely with the organization's mission. An example might be animal lovers who volunteer to raise money for the local animal shelter, because they see the work of the organization as an extension of their own passion for animals.

People's self-image is often improved when the community's image of them is enhanced. For many volunteers, being known and recognized as a successful fundraiser is rewarding because it raises their image in the community and their self-image. Volunteers also feel a great deal of satisfaction by knowing their fundraising skills have enabled an organization they care about to continue or expand their programs. As Stebbins says, volunteerism is often looked at as serious leisure, a form of recreation for the volunteers. Many successful fundraising volunteers hold responsible, demanding positions within their companies, and offering to serve as a volunteer is viewed as a pleasant diversion from their routine tasks. Evidence of this is the success of United Way's Loaned Executive Program. Companies will loan volunteers from businesses and corporations to United Way for several weeks, where they hone their fundraising skills while working on the annual United Way campaign. Finally, the organization should not overlook the possibility of financial return for the volunteers. The networking done at volunteer meetings and the community recognition has often helped successful fundraisers gain new business for their companies. For example, a banker or accountant might serve on a nonprofit's annual corporate appeal or capital campaign drive and develop a relationship with the organization that could lead to a business relationship.

The social rewards listed by Stebbins are equally important for staff to remember. Social attraction and group accomplishment can also be high motivating factors for volunteers. The ability to network and associate with clients of the organization and other volunteers can be socially rewarding. Often organizations assign business people to roles on the Board that appear to be in line with the person's career status. Therefore, they assign all of the bankers and

IN THE REAL WORLD

Avoiding Conflicts of Interest

An entrepreneurial owner of a small construction company provided many hours of service on the Board of a local charity. When it was time for the organization to engage a builder for a large capital project it was contemplating, the volunteer said he would not bid for the job because he felt there would be a perceived conflict of interest because of his Board position, but would provide his services to develop a request for proposals for a construction company, meet with potential bidders, and help guide the project in his role as Facility Committee Chair. Although there was no direct benefit to this volunteer from the building project of the nonprofit, a fellow Board member, and owner of a large retail chain, engaged the volunteer to do several projects for his company, having been impressed with the work this volunteer did for the charity.

Volunteers Have
Many Talents and Interests

One community volunteer who worked for a bank relates that she was always asked to serve on the finance committee of every Board on which she served. In reality, this volunteer really enjoyed academic pursuits and fundraising. The organization that was the recipient of most of her volunteer time was a local college that invited her to serve on the academic standards committee and involved her in its annual corporate appeal.

accountants to the finance committee, the architects to the facility committee, and the PR professionals to the marketing committee. In reality, these volunteers may have other interests and would find it extremely rewarding to be able to work with the members of the local symphony orchestra on developing the season program, serve on the ethics committee of a local hospital, or raise money for the human service organization that serves the hungry.

Pride in group accomplishment should not be overlooked either. In a capital campaign, it is particularly noted that the team of volunteers feels a great sense of accomplishing monumental feats by working together. In all volunteer fundraising activities, the role of the individual volunteer as part of the group should be emphasized. While working, for example, on an annual corporate appeal, volunteers should know that there are also student volunteers conducting a phone-a-thon, office volunteers stuffing a mail appeal, and another group of volunteers organizing the annual gala dinner dance. Feeling part of a larger whole makes the volunteers feel that they can make a difference by offering their own unique skills and contacts.

Working with Corporate Volunteers

Working with other volunteers differs from working with fundraising volunteers mainly in the type of people who volunteer for fundraising assignments. Fundraising volunteers often come from the ranks of the business community and include key community leaders and often younger up-and-coming professionals seeking the experience and networking opportunities that fundraising provides.

Why do corporations allow and even encourage their employees to take numerous hours away from work time to get involved with nonprofit organizations? There are several reasons why a business would want its employees involved. Many companies strive to be good corporate citizens, and volunteerism is a perfect way to support their community. Knowing there is no lack of nonprofits looking for people to help them with their fundraising activities, companies often actually help employees find a good match for their interests. Businesses may also view volunteer involvement by their employees as a good marketing tactic.

Understanding what has previously been said about networking opportunities by employees, a company may encourage its employees to get involved in nonprofit work in order to make business contacts. Another reason businesses may encourage volunteer involvement by their employees is to substitute for cash contributions. In fact, many communities encourage businesses to contribute dollars, gifts in kind, and volunteer hours to the nonprofits in their communities. In Las Vegas, Nevada, for example, the Business Community Investment Council (BCIC) has initiated a two percent club, challenging local businesses to give two percent of their pre-tax profits to charitable organizations, in a combination of cash, gifts in kind, or volunteer hours. In many communities, leadership programs encourage Board service and volunteerism from up-and-coming community leaders. This influx of new corporate volunteers into the fundraising

In her column in **Contributions,** *Kay Sprinkel Grace lists 10 things organizations need to know about recruiting younger people for their Boards as follows:*

1. *Focus.* The organization needs to have well-run Board meetings.

2. *Relevance.* Its mission must be relevant to community needs.

3. *Action.* Young people want to be change agents, not just talk about issues.

4. *Impact.* The program must have measurable results.

5. *Involvement.* Young people want hands-on experience with the organization's program.

6. *Connections.* They seek the ability to network and learn from other Board members.

7. *Fun.* The organization shouldn't make Board meetings too serious.

8. *Growth.* Young Board members can benefit from having a mentor who can help teach them how to be good Board members.

9. *Leverage.* Board service can enhance the personal lives of Board members; they want to use the time spent in volunteering to learn new skills that will enhance their lives.

10. *Skills.* Remember that younger Board members will have their own set of skills that older members can learn from them, such as technology and marketing.

arena means that nonprofits will need to be prepared to work with a new breed of corporate leaders, in particular young professionals. Younger people are often looking for volunteer opportunities, but the organization must be prepared to deal with this next generation of volunteers.

Whether these younger volunteers are Board members or fundraising volunteers, all of these points are good to consider. Corporate leaders and younger volunteers share a lot of these issues. Organizations that are successful in recruiting and retaining corporate volunteers and young professionals usually have some things in common:

- They have a well-understood mission and a high community image.

- They plan their meetings at times that are convenient to the business world and do not take volunteers away from their families.

- They have key community leaders involved in their fundraising activities that attract other volunteers.

- They communicate well with their volunteers and provide opportunities for them to work with other volunteers.

- They provide opportunities for volunteers to become involved in the program.

- They make volunteering fun.

A Phenomenon in Some Communities Affecting Volunteerism

Some communities, particularly those in the northeast United States, have a unique group that gets involved with organizations that are planning capital campaigns. These groups are usually called the Capital Campaign Review Board for the community. Although these Review Boards have no legal authority, they can be powerful in their communities because they approve or disapprove all capital campaigns that are conducted in their community. In a survey done by this author, it was determined that most of these Boards consist of volunteers who hold key leadership positions in their community, heads of banks and other business and industry leaders, foundation executives, and sometimes political figures. In communities where there is a Capital Campaign Review Board, it is critical for the nonprofit to have this Board's approval for several reasons. First, many businesses in the community will not financially support a capital campaign that has not been approved by the Review Board. Second, it will be practically impossible for a nonapproved campaign to recruit volunteer leadership from any of the major businesses in that community. One of the things the nonprofits in communities where there is a Review Board say that they like about this process is the certainty that if they have their campaign approved, they will be able to recruit key community leaders to get involved in their campaign.

What Staff Can Expect from Volunteers

The staff of the nonprofit, especially the Chief Development Officers, have a huge responsibility to recruit, train, and retain good fundraising volunteers, but they also have a right to expect some things from the volunteers involved in their programs.

Volunteers should be expected to maintain confidentiality of information learned through their volunteer service, complete assignments on time, present the organization in a positive and professional manner, and disclose any conflicts of interest they might have regarding the organization. Many organizations ask volunteers, especially Board members, to sign an agreement outlining the expectations of both the organization and the volunteer. Development staff will bear the primary responsibility of managing the fundraising volunteer program. If the organization has a volunteer coordinator, this person is generally responsible for program and office volunteers, but because fundraising volunteers will be involved in work only the Development Office can fully manage, these volunteers should report to the Chief Development Officer.

TIPS & TECHNIQUES

Managing the fundraising volunteer program can be an exciting task for a development professional as well as carrying an important responsibility. The development officer who is most successful at managing fundraising volunteers will follow these guidelines:

- Develop clear expectations for all fundraising volunteers, including the obligation to make their own gift first.

- Be sensitive to the needs and motivations of volunteers.

- Always act in a professional manner with volunteers.

- Plan meetings and activities at times and locations that are convenient for volunteers, which may require meeting in the volunteer's office or at early morning hours.

- Provide volunteers with the information they need.

- Never ask a volunteer to do anything that is unethical or illegal.

- Train and educate the volunteers about the entire philanthropic process, not just the tasks in which they will be involved.

- Teach volunteers that their highest obligation is to the donor.

Further Reading

Grace, Kay Sprinkel. "Ten Things You Should Know About Recruiting Younger People for Your Board." *Contributions*, September–October 2004.

Lee, Jarene Frances. "Is Your Staff Ready for Volunteers?" *Contributions,* September–October 2004.

Stebbins, Robert A. "Volunteering: A Serious Leisure Perspective." *Nonprofit and Voluntary Sector Quarterly,* Volume 25, Number 2, June 1996.

CHAPTER 8

Getting Started

After reading this chapter, you will be able to:

- Determine your organization's fundraising volunteer needs.
- Develop position descriptions for the fundraising volunteers to be recruited.
- Develop a Fundraising Volunteer Recruitment and Management Plan.

Determining Volunteer Needs

Once the organization has decided to work with volunteer fundraisers, the first step is analyzing the volunteer needs. Using the formula previously discussed, remember that volunteers who will make solicitation calls should not be assigned to more than five to seven calls at a time. In order, therefore, to determine the number of volunteers needed, first estimate the number of prospects to be solicited and then divide by five to determine the approximate number of volunteers needed (see Exhibit 8.1 at the end of this chapter). Volunteers can be used in many aspects of fundraising, so a plan will need to be developed for the entire fundraising program, including Board development.

Defining Volunteer Responsibilities

Now that the volunteer needs have been determined, it will be necessary to develop volunteer position descriptions for each category of volunteers that will be used. Remember that different skills will be required, and volunteers and staff will have different expectations for the various volunteers involved. For example, a volunteer who will help research grants will need different skills than the volunteer chair of the capital campaign.

The Development Office should have a manual, both in hard copy and electronic form, containing all of the volunteer position descriptions so that when volunteers are to be recruited, the appropriate position description can be pulled from the manual to be included in the volunteer recruitment packet. Position descriptions should be reviewed with volunteers who have filled those positions at the end of each year to see if the descriptions accurately reflect the roles that volunteers filled. After a campaign, event, or activity has been completed, a debriefing should always take place, at which time volunteers can discuss their roles and determine what changes are recommended for future campaigns, events, and activities.

Using the same model shown in Exhibit 8.1 to develop the volunteer positions needed, the organization can then determine which position descriptions are current and which need to be developed or revised and use the checklist in Exhibit 8.2 at the end of this chapter to keep position descriptions current.

Identifying the Type of Volunteers Needed

Next, the organization should list the qualities needed by each of the various volunteers. Along with analyzing the skills needed, it may also be important to list the demographics of the type of volunteers the organization is seeking. This will be critical in Board development but may also prove helpful in other areas. For example, the Development Committee or the Campaign Cabinet will need to accurately reflect the organization's constituency (e.g., is it geographically diverse, ethnically diverse, gender diverse?). Again, using the same list of volunteer opportunities that has already been developed, it will be necessary to develop a volunteer profile for each area in which the organization will be using volunteers. The grid shown in Exhibit 8.3 at the end of this chapter suggests some qualities needed in various areas. Remember that commitment to the organization's mission should be of primary concern for *all* volunteers.

These suggestions may need to be refined by each organization, and remember, some attributes are more important in some volunteers than they are in others. For example, leadership qualities and financial ability become more important the higher in the leadership hierarchy a volunteer is placed. The chair of the capital campaign will generally need stronger leadership qualities, more community recognition, and greater financial ability than the rest of the Campaign Cabinet. The chair of a special event may need better organizational skills than members of the special event committee, and so on. Also, the skills required from volunteers will depend on the availability of experienced, skilled development staff. For example, most of the volunteers will not need writing skills assuming that the development staff will write fundraising materials for the volunteers. If there is no development staff to fill this role, volunteers may be required to write their own fundraising appeal letters, and this skill will need to be added to the list of requirements for that volunteer position.

Developing a List of Potential Volunteers

Once the list of qualities and the position description are in place, the next step is to list all of the areas in which volunteers need to be recruited and then develop a list of potential volunteers who possess the qualities needed to fill these volunteer roles. As already discussed, there are many places where volunteers can be found. When contacting civic and professional organizations, volunteer centers, leadership programs, or local businesses, the organization should have a list of volunteer roles and the position descriptions for those roles in hand.

Another tactic that can be used to develop a pool of qualified fundraising volunteers is to have the list of volunteer positions, qualities required, and position descriptions in hand and then conduct a brainstorming session at a Board meeting, Advisory Board meeting, or Development Committee meeting to see how many names can be added to the list of prospective volunteers. It will be critical to assign someone to contact the volunteers—a staff member, Board member, or another volunteer. A grid like that shown in Exhibit 8.4 at the end of this chapter can be used to develop a volunteer recruitment plan.

Preparing Volunteer Recruitment Materials

Next, the organization needs to prepare recruitment packets to review with the prospective volunteer. Each volunteer position will need different materials. In general, the higher the volunteer position, the more information the volunteer will require. In a capital campaign, volunteers should receive a three- to four-inch notebook so they can put all of the meeting agendas, minutes of meetings, campaign plan and timeline, budget, and other campaign materials all in one place. Staff should remind campaign cabinet members to bring notebooks along to all campaign cabinet meetings and provide hole-punched reports and other items for volunteers to place into their notebooks. In fact, if a campaign secretary has been appointed, this person can actually replace old pages and insert new ones for the cabinet members during the meeting. It is amazing how a well-run organization will succeed in recruiting and retaining good volunteers because they really appreciate the fact that the organization makes their job easier by providing amenities such as these.

This notebook is usually given later in the recruitment process, once the volunteer agrees to serve. However, during the first recruitment visit, a folder with the case for support, an abbreviated campaign plan, campaign timeline, and position descriptions for the role the volunteer is being asked to consider should be given to prospective campaign cabinet members. Volunteers for special events and the annual campaign should also be given a recruitment packet at the initial recruitment meeting and then a notebook once they have agreed to serve. A checklist of materials volunteers typically need is shown in Exhibit 8.5 at the end of this chapter.

Recruiting Volunteers

The organization is now ready to start recruiting its volunteers. As with major donor solicitations, it will be important to have the right people making the ask. Volunteer recruitment for key positions should be handled as carefully as a major gift call. If the position is a high-level one, a team of two or more people is best to make the "ask," usually the chief executive of the organization and a key volunteer. Prepare the materials in advance, know what the organization wants and expects from the volunteer, rehearse possible scenarios in advance of the meeting, and have the meeting carefully arranged. As with a major gift call, the volunteer should be visited at his or her office or home. A volunteer recruitment packet containing the materials determined to be needed in explaining the volunteer role should be prepared and reviewed by the team that will be calling on the prospective volunteer.

The recruitment team should be prepared to discuss the project and the timeline for completing the volunteer assignment, the organization and its mission (particularly if the prospective volunteer is not intimately familiar with the organization), and the volunteer position description. They should also be prepared to handle objections the volunteer may have. It is crucial to have a timeline and know how much of the volunteer's time will be required. Time restrictions may be one of the volunteers' major objections, but often once they see the organizational chart for the campaign or project, they will see that a whole team is working on this project and their responsibility will be shared with other volunteers. This is often enough to alleviate the fear that they cannot take on a project of this magnitude. It will be important to recruit volunteers from the top down, because once the leader is in place, it will be much easier to involve other volunteers, particularly if the top volunteer is a well-known and respected community leader.

Volunteer leadership will recruit volunteers who will be working in positions other than leadership roles in the campaign or appeal. In a capital campaign, for example, the Campaign Chair or Chairs should be recruited first, and then they will help identify others who might serve on the campaign cabinet with them. Once all of the Division Chairs (who will be cabinet members) are in place, they can brainstorm with staff and the rest of the volunteers about potential members for each of the committees. The volunteer recruitment process is much less intimidating when taken step by step.

Developing the Orientation and Training Program

Once volunteers are recruited, the organization needs to develop its plan for the orientation, training, and education of these volunteers. The plan needs to include determining the time and place for each training event, the leaders who will be involved in training and education, and the volunteers who will be oriented, trained, and educated. The grid in Exhibit 8.6 at the end of this chapter can be used to establish a training and education calendar.

Working with the Volunteers

The development staff has the awesome responsibility of being the guardian of one of the organization's most precious commodities—its volunteers. Remember that volunteers have expectations of the organization and that to keep good volunteers, staff must be sensitive to the needs of the volunteers, while asking volunteers to stretch themselves to greatness. The volunteer who feels challenged in the volunteer role, who feels like a part of a greater mission, and who enjoys the volunteer experience is the volunteer who will do well at fundraising, will stay involved with the organization, and will recruit others to become involved.

To summarize the role of the development staff, a checklist for staff to follow includes:

- Training other staff members about the importance of supporting volunteers.

- Always looking, talking, and acting in a professional manner.

- Providing volunteers with the tools they need to do their jobs.

- Providing training and education for volunteers.

- Helping volunteers understand the process and psychology of philanthropy.

- Inviting volunteers to stretch to new heights in the volunteer work they provide.

- Teaching volunteers about the ethics of fundraising.

Acknowledging and Recognizing Volunteers

The final step in the volunteer management process is acknowledgment and recognition of volunteers. Fundraising volunteers are usually highly motivated people who will most often be more motivated by recognition than other volunteers. Therefore, these volunteers should be publicly recognized and given tokens of appreciation that will be visible in their office or home. Like all volunteers, they must be thanked for their service to the organization. A plan for recognition and acknowledgment should be part of the volunteer management program. This plan should include a timeline and budget for recognition items.

A typical plan might include the following ways of thanking and recognizing fundraising volunteers:

Acknowledgment:

- Thank-you letter—computer generated, signed by the Chief Development Officer.

- ○ Handwritten thank-you note, signed by the chief volunteer for the appeal or campaign in which the volunteer has worked.
- ○ Thank-you phone call from the Chief Executive Officer of the organization.
- ○ Verbal thanks for special achievements and at the conclusion of the volunteer's service.

Recognition:

- ○ Listing in quarterly newsletter.
- ○ Listing in annual report.
- ○ Listing in special campaign newsletter.
- ○ Paid ad in local newspaper.
- ○ Announcement of volunteer's accomplishments at campaign meetings.
- ○ Mementos such as plaques, paperweight, coffee mugs, etc.
- ○ Special parking privileges at the organization's facility.
- ○ Nomination for community awards such as the Association of Fundraising Professionals' Volunteer Fundraiser of the Year Award at a local AFP chapter's National Philanthropy Day celebration.
- ○ Consideration for a higher level of involvement with the organization (e.g., a Team Leader might move into the position of Annual Appeal Vice Chair or a Capital Campaign Chair might receive a nomination to the Board of Directors).

Although there are numerous ways fundraising volunteers can be rewarded, remember that a simple thank you is always appreciated and that many types of recognition are not high-cost items. The organization that gives its volunteers appropriate acknowledgment and recognition is the organization that will be most successful in keeping volunteers involved for many years.

EXHIBIT 8.1

Volunteer Needs Analysis

Volunteer Fundraisers	Number of Volunteers Needed	Number of Volunteers Currently Involved	Number of Volunteers to be Recruited
Advisory Board Members			
Board Members			
Development Committee Members			
Volunteers to help develop the Case for Support			
Volunteer to help identify potential donors			
Cultivation Events—Hosts			
Volunteers to help develop or expand the Planned Giving program			
Volunteers to be interviewed in a planning study for a proposed capital/endowment campaign			
Capital Campaign—Chair(s)			
Capital Campaign Cabinet			
Capital Campaign Committee Members for various divisions			
Annual Appeal—Chair(s)			
Annual Fund—Corporate Appeal Chairs			
Annual Fund—Corporate Appeal Team Leaders			
Annual Fund—Corporate Appeal Team Members			

continued on the next page

Volunteer Fundraisers	Number of Volunteers Needed	Number of Volunteers Currently Involved	Number of Volunteers to be Recruited
Annual Fund—Community Appeal Chair(s)			
Annual Fund—Community Appeal Team Captains			
Annual Fund—Community Appeal Team Members			
Annual Appeal— Phonathon Chairs			
Annual Appeal— Phonathon Team Captains			
Annual Appeal— Phonathon Team Members			
Annual Appeal— Mailing Letter Signer(s)			
Annual Appeal— Mailing Stuffers			
Special Event # 1—Chair(s)			
Special Event # 1— Committee Members			
Special Event # 1— Volunteers			
Special Event # 2—Chair(s)			
Special Event # 2— Committee Members			
Special Event # 2— Volunteers			
Grants—Researchers			
Grants—Writers			
Development Office Support			
Other Volunteers: List Areas of Need			

EXHIBIT 8.2

Volunteer Position Descriptions

Volunteer Fundraisers	Position Description in Manual	Position Description Has Been Reviewed with Current Volunteers	Position Description Needs to be Revised
Advisory Board Members			
Board Members			
Development Committee Members			
Volunteers to help develop the Case for Support			
Volunteer to help identify potential donors			
Cultivation Events—Hosts			
Volunteers to help develop or expand the Planned Giving program			
Volunteers to be interviewed in a planning study for a proposed capital/endowment campaign			
Capital Campaign—Chair(s)			
Capital Campaign Cabinet			
Capital Campaign Committee Members for various divisions			
Annual Appeal—Chair(s)			
Annual Fund—Corporate Appeal Chairs			
Annual Fund—Corporate Appeal Team Leaders			

continued on the next page

Volunteer Fundraisers	Position Description in Manual	Position Description Has Been Reviewed with Current Volunteers	Position Description Needs to be Revised
Annual Fund—Corporate Appeal Team Members			
Annual Fund—Community Appeal Chair(s)			
Annual Fund—Community Appeal Team Captains			
Annual Fund—Community Appeal Team Members			
Annual Appeal— Phonathon Chairs			
Annual Appeal— Phonathon Team Captains			
Annual Appeal—Phonathon Team Members			
Annual Appeal—Mailing Letter Signer(s)			
Annual Appeal— Mailing Stuffers			
Special Event # 1—Chair(s)			
Special Event # 1— Committee Members			
Special Event # 1— Volunteers			
Special Event # 2—Chair(s)			
Special Event # 2— Committee Members			
Special Event # 2—Volunteers			
Grants—Researchers			
Grants—Writers			
Development Office Support			
Other Volunteers: List Areas of Need			

EXHIBIT 8.3

Volunteer Qualities Assessment

Volunteer Fundraisers	Ethnic Diversity	Geographic Diversity	Gender Diversity	Other Diversity Issues	Community Contacts	Organizational Skills	Writing Skills	Speaking Skills	Technical Skills (computer skills, Planned Giving Expert, etc.)	Financial Ability	Community Recognition	Leadership Skills
Advisory Board Members	✓	✓	✓	✓	✓					✓	✓	✓
Board Members	✓	✓	✓	✓	✓			✓	✓	✓	✓	✓
Development Committee Members	✓	✓	✓	✓	✓	✓		✓	✓	✓	✓	✓
Volunteers to help develop the Case for Support					✓		✓	✓			✓	
Volunteer to help identify potential donors					✓							
Cultivation Events—Hosts					✓	✓		✓		✓	✓	
Volunteers to help develop or expand the Planned Giving program					✓			✓	✓	✓	✓	
Volunteers to be interviewed in a planning study for a proposed capital/endowment campaign					✓	✓				✓	✓	✓
Capital Campaign—Chair(s)					✓	✓		✓		✓	✓	✓
Capital Campaign Cabinet	✓	✓	✓	✓	✓	✓		✓	✓	✓	✓	✓
Capital Campaign Committee Members for various divisions	✓	✓	✓	✓	✓				✓	✓	✓	
Annual Appeal—Chair(s)					✓	✓		✓		✓	✓	✓
Annual Fund—Corporate Appeal Chairs					✓	✓		✓		✓	✓	✓
Annual Fund—Corporate Appeal Team Leaders	✓	✓	✓	✓	✓	✓				✓	✓	✓
Annual Fund—Corporate Appeal Team Members		✓	✓	✓	✓	✓			✓		✓	✓
Annual Fund—Community Appeal Chair(s)					✓	✓		✓		✓	✓	✓

continued on the next page

163

Volunteer Qualities Assessment (continued)

Volunteer Fundraisers	Ethnic Diversity	Geographic Diversity	Gender Diversity	Other Diversity Issues	Community Contacts	Organizational Skills	Writing Skills	Speaking Skills	Technical Skills (computer skills, Planned Giving Expert, etc.)	Financial Ability	Community Recognition	Leadership Skills
Annual Fund—Community Appeal Team Captains	✓	✓	✓	✓	✓	✓		✓		✓	✓	✓
Annual Fund—Community Appeal Team Members	✓	✓	✓	✓	✓			✓		✓		
Annual Appeal—Phonathon Chairs						✓		✓		✓	✓	✓
Annual Appeal—Phonathon Team Captains						✓		✓				✓
Annual Appeal—Phonathon Team Members								✓				
Annual Appeal—Mailing Letter Signer(s)					✓		✓	✓		✓	✓	
Annual Appeal—Mailing Stuffers						✓			✓			
Special Event # 1—Chair(s)					✓	✓		✓		✓	✓	✓
Special Event # 1—Committee Members					✓	✓			✓		✓	✓
Special Event # 1—Volunteers						✓			✓			
Special Event # 2—Chair(s)					✓	✓		✓		✓	✓	✓
Special Event # 2—Committee Members					✓	✓			✓		✓	✓
Special Event # 2—Volunteers						✓			✓			
Grants—Researchers						✓			✓			
Grants—Writers						✓	✓	✓				
Development Office Support							✓		✓			
Other Volunteers: List Areas of Need												

Volunteer Recruitment Plan

Volunteer Position	Volunteer Prospect	Person Who Will Invite This Prospect	Recruitment Materials Prepared	Target Date for Recruitment	Result

EXHIBIT 8.5

Volunteer Recruitment Materials

Volunteer Fundraisers	Case for Support	Budget—Org. or Project	Bylaws	Org. Chart	Position Description	Project Timeline	Org Brochure, Annual Report, etc.	Dev. Plan	Notebook When Recruited
Advisory Board Members	✓	Org.	✓	Org.	✓		✓	✓	✓
Board Members	✓	Org.	✓	Org.	✓		✓	✓	✓
Development Committee Members	✓	Org.		Comm. Dev. Org.	✓		✓	✓	✓
Volunteers to help develop the Case for Support	✓	✓		✓		✓	✓	✓	
Volunteer to help identify potential donors	✓				✓	✓	✓	✓	
Cultivation Events—Hosts	✓				✓		✓		
Volunteers to help develop or expand the Planned Giving program	✓	✓			✓		✓	✓	
Volunteers to be interviewed in a planning study for a proposed capital/endowment campaign	✓	Project		Campaign		✓	✓		
Capital Campaign—Chair(s)	✓	Project & Campaign		Campaign	✓	✓	✓		✓
Capital Campaign Cabinet	✓	Project & Campaign		Campaign	✓	✓	✓		✓
Capital Campaign Committee Members for various divisions	✓	Project & Campaign		Campaign	✓	✓	✓		
Annual Appeal—Chair(s)	✓			Appeal	✓	✓	✓	✓	✓
Annual Fund—Corporate Appeal Chairs	✓			Appeal	✓	✓	✓		✓

Annual Fund—Corporate Appeal Team Leaders	✓		Appeal	✓	✓	✓			
Annual Fund—Corporate Appeal Team Members	✓		Appeal	✓	✓	✓			
Annual Fund—Community Appeal Chair(s)	✓		Appeal	✓	✓	✓			✓
Annual Fund—Community Appeal Team Captains	✓		Appeal	✓	✓	✓			
Annual Fund—Community Appeal Team Members	✓		Appeal	✓	✓	✓			
Annual Appeal—Phonathon Chairs	✓		Appeal	✓	✓	✓			✓
Annual Appeal—Phonathon Team Captains	✓		Appeal	✓	✓	✓			
Annual Appeal—Phonathon Team Members	✓			✓	✓	Script			
Annual Appeal—Mailing Letter Signer(s)	✓		Appeal	✓	✓	✓			
Annual Appeal—Mailing Stuffers	✓			✓	✓	✓			
Special Event # 1—Chair(s)	✓	Event	Event	✓	✓	✓			✓
Special Event # 1—Committee Members	✓	Event	Event	✓	✓	✓			✓
Special Event # 1—Volunteers	✓			✓	✓	✓			
Special Event # 2—Chair(s)	✓	Event	Event	✓	✓	✓			✓
Special Event # 2—Committee Members	✓	Event	Event	✓	✓	✓			✓
Special Event # 2—Volunteers	✓			✓	✓	✓			
Grants—Researchers	✓	Program	Org.	✓	✓	✓		✓	✓
Grants—Writers	✓	Program	Org.	✓	✓	✓	Prior grants	✓	✓
Development Office Support	✓		Org. & Dev Office	✓	✓	✓		✓	
Other Volunteers: List Areas of Need									

167

EXHIBIT 8.6

Volunteer Training Schedule

Volunteer Fundraisers	Orientation: Date, Time, Location, Leaders	Training: Date, Time, Location, Leaders	Education Sessions
Advisory Board Members	Within one month of joining Advisory Board	Only if involved in campaign or appeal	Once a year
Board Members	Within one month of joining Board	Only if involved in campaign or appeal	One 15-minute session at each board meeting, annual retreat
Development Committee Members	Within one month of joining Committee	As needed depending on involvement in campaigns, appeals	One 15-minute session at each committee meeting, annual strategy session
Volunteers to help develop the Case for Support	When invited to help with case	None required	None required
Volunteers to help identify potential donors	When invited to assist with prospect identification	At initial screening session	None required
Cultivation Events—Hosts	Two months before cultivation events	None required	None required
Volunteers to help develop or expand the Planned Giving program	Within a month after joining the committee	None required if experienced in Planned Giving	As new Planned Giving techniques or instruments are introduced
Volunteers to be interviewed in a planning study for a proposed capital/endowment campaign	None required	None required	None required
Capital Campaign—Chair(s)	Within one month of agreeing to serve	Before the Leadership solicitations are begun	None required
Capital Campaign Cabinet	Within one month of agreeing to serve	Each member to be trained before their division begins solicitations	None required

Capital Campaign Committee Members for various divisions	Within one month of agreeing to serve	Each member to be trained before their division begins solicitations	None required
Annual Appeal—Phonathon Chairs	Within one month of agreeing to serve	First night of phoning	None required
Annual Appeal—Phonathon Team Captains	Within one month of agreeing to serve	One month before recruiting team members, and first night of phoning	None required
Annual Appeal—Phonathon Team Members	Within one month of agreeing to serve	First night of phoning	None required
Annual Appeal—Mailing Letter Signer(s)	Within one month of agreeing to serve	None required	None required
Annual Appeal—Mailing Stuffers	Within one month of agreeing to serve	Two weeks before mailing	None required
Special Event # 1—Chair(s)	Within one month of agreeing to serve	None required unless there will be sponsorships or other solicitations	None required
Special Event # 1—Committee Members	Within one month of agreeing to serve	None required unless there will be sponsorships or other solicitations	None required
Special Event # 1—Volunteers	Within one month of agreeing to serve	One week before event	None required
Special Event # 2—Chair(s)	Within one month of agreeing to serve	None required unless there will be sponsorships or other solicitations	None required
Special Event # 2—Committee Members	Within one month of agreeing to serve	None required unless there will be sponsorships or other solicitations	None required
Special Event # 2—Volunteers	Within one month of agreeing to serve	One week before event	None required
Grants—Researchers	Within one month of agreeing to serve	Two weeks before research is started	As new programs are introduced
Grants—Writers	Within one month of agreeing to serve	Two months before grants writing starts	As new programs are introduced
Development Office Support	Within one month of agreeing to serve	Two weeks before service begins	Annual retreat with staff
Other Volunteers: List Areas of Need			

Index